KATE BUSH

SONG BY SONG

JOHN VAN DER KISTE

D1603595

FONTHILL

Fonthill Media Language Policy

Fonthill Media publishes in the international English language market. One language edition is published worldwide. As there are minor differences in spelling and presentation, especially with regard to American English and British English, a policy is necessary to define which form of English to use. The Fonthill Policy is to use the form of English native to the author. John Van der Kiste was born and educated in the UK; therefore British English has been adopted in this publication.

Fonthill Media Limited
Fonthill Media LLC
www.fonthillmedia.com
office@fonthillmedia.com

First published in the United Kingdom and the United States of America 2021

British Library Cataloguing in Publication Data:
A catalogue record for this book is available from the British Library

Copyright © John Van der Kiste 2021

ISBN 978-1-78155-824-9

Typeset in 10pt on 13pt Sabon
Printed and bound in England

Acknowledgements

Particular thanks are due to Ian Herne for the exchanges we have enjoyed on the subject of Kate and her music by e-mail while I was writing the book; to Francis Jansen, Michael Guth, Bart Lienard, James Russell, and Paul Thomas for supplying photographs and scans of material; to my editors at Fonthill Media, George Kalchev, Jay Slater, and Josh Greenland; and to my wife, Kim, for her support and encouragement in reading the material.

Contents

Author's Note

All chart positions given are for the UK unless stated otherwise.

Kate Bush's records initially appeared in Britain, Europe, and other countries on the EMI label, and from 2011 on her own label Fish People. The EMI catalogue was subsequently transferred to Parlophone and more recent reissues came out on the latter. In America, they were first released on EMI America, then Columbia from 1989, while in Canada they were initially on Harvest, EMI America from 1983, and Capitol from 1989.

Timings for each track are approximate, and inevitably subject to minor variation from one source to another.

Introduction

In 1975, the number of successful female singer-songwriters on both sides of the Atlantic could almost be counted on the fingers of one hand. Only two, Carole King and Joni Mitchell, ever enjoyed the popularity that had given each of them a major hit single or two and a string of best-selling albums in Britain. Of the others, Loretta Lynn was always regarded primarily as a country performer, while the chart successes of Bobbie Gentry and Nina Simone rested largely on a few hits written by others. Laura Nyro and Judee Sill were widely respected but had little appeal beyond their dedicated but small fan bases, while Sandy Denny was remembered less for her solo career than as vocalist with Fairport Convention and briefly Fotheringay. Moreover, all but the last-named were American or Canadian. In Britain, neither Catherine Howe, once described as 'a Kate Bush before her time', nor Jaki Whitren ever amassed more than a small cult following, while the newly-emerging Joan Armatrading's day was yet to come. Meanwhile, the American-born, but British-based female singer and musician (bass guitar) with the highest profile in Britain at that time, Suzi Quatro, was writing her own B-sides but would never be known primarily as a singer-songwriter.

This was also the year that saw the initial blossoming of the talent from a seventeen-year-old performer who would become Britain's foremost name in the field. Born in Bexleyheath, Kent, on 30 July 1958, and brought up in the family home at East Welling, Catherine (later Kate) Bush came from an artistic background. Her mother, Hannah, had long been a traditional Irish dancer, while her father, Robert, a doctor by profession, was an amateur songwriter and pianist, and played the church organ. She had two elder brothers; John was a poet, photographer and occasional novelist, while Paddy was a musician and musical instrument maker who worked for the English Folk Dance and Song Society, and regularly played for dancers in local folk clubs. As there was always an eclectic diet of music in the family home, the youngest member was regularly exposed to folk, the classics, the American songbook, and something of the rock and pop world. The first album she bought was Simon & Garfunkel's *Bridge Over Troubled Water*, and other favourite artists from her early teenage days included Elton John, David Bowie, Roxy Music, and King Crimson.

While studying at St Joseph's Convent Grammar School, Abbey Wood, South London, she learnt piano and violin, and played the organ in a barn behind their house. In her early teens, she began writing songs, showing a remarkable grasp of melodic structure, intricate chords, and ambitious lyrical themes, far removed from the standard three- or four-chord lovey-dovey pop on which many of her (mostly male) peers cut their songwriting teeth. Early in her career, she was dismissive about much of the music that was around, particularly the mundane lyrical content—'purely romantic bubblegum,' she called it. 'Just talking about boy-meets-girl.'[1]

Ricky Hopper, a friend of John Bush who worked in the music industry, was struck by the quality of her early work, and in 1972, he tried to interest music publishers and record companies in her early demo tapes, but without success. A little later, he persuaded David Gilmour of Pink Floyd, a friend since their days together at Cambridge University, to listen. David knew that the songs were not saleable as they stood, but that she had remarkable gifts and potential. He recruited a couple of other musicians and arranged for her to record some better quality demos, and brought them to the attention of arranger and producer Andrew Powell. Ironically, it later emerged that when she first met David, she had never heard anything recorded by Pink Floyd, an omission she soon rectified.

In the summer of 1976, she concluded a deal with EMI, to include Britain, Europe, and Canada, but not the United States, where EMI America would have a first option without any obligation to release her material. Mindful of the 'child star syndrome' and anxious not to push her too early, the label managers decided against sending her into the studio immediately, but first allowed her time to develop her art, studying dance, mime, and vocal technique as well as writing more songs at her own pace. The period between signing the deal and recording her first album also included a few months of rehearsing at West Wickham and playing at London pubs fronting the KT Bush Band, also comprising Brian Bath on guitar, Del Palmer on bass guitar, and Vic King on drums. A set of about twenty songs, including material by Kate and a selection of covers, among them 'Honky Tonk Women', 'Nutbush City Limits', 'I Heard It Through the Grapevine', 'Tracks of My Tears', and 'Come Together', saw them playing twenty gigs between April and June 1977, after which EMI decided she was ready for the next stage.

Sessions for the first album took place at AIR Studios, London, over six weeks in July and August. Kate particularly wanted her band to take part but Andrew Powell, who was producing, insisted that she should use experienced session musicians with whom he had previously worked instead. The core of the band therefore consisted of Ian Bairnson on guitar, David Paton on bass guitar, Duncan Mackay on keyboards, and Stuart Elliott on drums. The two former had been members of Pilot, the others part of Steve Harley and Cockney Rebel; coincidentally, both groups, each signed to EMI, had had consecutive chart-toppers just over two years earlier with 'January' and 'Make Me Smile (Come Up and See Me)' respectively.

Two songs from the 1975 demo tapes, 'The Man with the Child in His Eyes' and 'The Saxophone Song', were considered of sufficient quality to add to the newer material, once strings had been added. Many more taped at the same time as those, but never officially released, were later bootlegged and subsequently uploaded on the internet, including 'Scares Me Silly (But It Gets Me Going),' 'Rinfy the Gypsy', 'Atlantis', 'Stranded on the Moonbase', and 'Organic Acid'. In 1986, an independent label in West Germany acquired a collection of early demos and her official German label, EMI-Electrola, licensed it for release. Test pressings were produced, but when Kate and her management were informed, release was halted.

Out of 120 songs she had available, a shortlist was made. One of the last she had written, 'Wuthering Heights', was scheduled as a single for November release but delayed, partly because of problems with the image on the picture sleeve and partly as it would have been considered commercial suicide to issue the debut of a new artist so close to Christmas. It appeared in January 1978 and within six weeks it had reached No. 1 in Britain, staying there for four weeks. The album, *The Kick Inside*, followed in February, and over the next two years spent sixty-six weeks on the album chart, peaking at No. 3. 'The Man with the Child in His Eyes', chosen as the second single from the album, reached No. 6.

After this almost instant success, an overzealous EMI put pressure on Kate to record a follow-up. Experiencing a financially troubled period—according to one source, in the second half of 1978 in Britain, the record division lost £14.6 million—it was keen to exploit its brightest hope.[2] Using mostly the same musicians again, and with Andrew Powell producing a second time, the next sessions took place that summer in a studio on the French Riviera. Seven songs from her vast collection plus three newly-written numbers were taped, and the result, 'Lionheart', was released in November. Although following its predecessor into the top ten, both singles, 'Hammer Horror' and 'Wow', fared less well, and critical reception was lukewarm. Kate herself admitted that it had been made too quickly, and she was dissatisfied with the finished product.

A few months earlier, she had been invited to open for Fleetwood Mac on the closing dates of their *Rumours* tour in August and September 1978. The idea of twenty-minute sets in American stadiums and arenas was not to her taste and she rejected the offer, having decided that when she began to perform live, it would be on her own terms or not at all. In April and May 1979, she played nineteen shows in Britain and eight in Europe, billed as the 'Tour of Life', with a ten-piece band, including Brian Bath and Del Palmer from the KT Bush Band, and her brother on mandolin and various other instruments. The performances involved seventeen costume changes for Kate, who played piano on a couple of numbers and also danced around the stage, singing through a wireless voice microphone, and a couple of poetry readings from her other brother, John. The opening date, a warm-up gig at Poole, was overshadowed by tragedy when the lighting engineer Bill Duffield was killed after falling from a stage and seating structure at the venue, and one of the closing dates at London was performed as a benefit for his family. Reviews of the show were positive, some even euphoric, with a reviewer from *Melody Maker* calling it 'the most magnificent spectacle ever encountered in the world of rock'. Nevertheless, the venture proved exhausting and unsuccessful from a financial point of view. Later she recalled that by the end, '[I] felt a terrific need to retreat as a person, because I felt that my sexuality, which in a way I hadn't really had a chance to explore myself, was being given to the world in a way which I found impersonal.'[3]

For more than thirty years afterwards, she said no to further touring and restricted her live concert appearances to participation in shows with others, mainly for charities. A four-track EP, *Kate Bush On Stage*, was released in August and reached No. 10. It was the first of several records she co-produced herself with Jon Kelly, who had been the engineer at AIR Studios on her first two albums. Most of her appearances on TV were carefully choreographed videos, rather than straightforward performances with a small band. In October, she recorded a Christmas special, *Kate*, at Pebble Mill Studios, Birmingham, broadcast on BBC TV on 28 December, featuring thirteen songs (two with Peter Gabriel) in a selection of pre-filmed sequences, dramatic in-studio set pieces, and straight performances at the piano. Around the same time, she and Paddy Bush contributed vocals to a charity single, 'Sing Children Sing' by Lesley Duncan, alongside Pete Townshend, Phil Lynott, and Joe and Vicki Brown, released in November. Early in 1980, she was heard prominently as backing vocalist on Peter Gabriel's first Top 10 hit 'Games Without Frontiers'.

That summer, she enjoyed further significant record success when her third album, *Never For Ever*, her first to feature synthesisers and drum machines, entered the British charts at No. 1, the first time a female British artist had topped the album charts. The two singles from it, 'Babooshka' and 'Army Dreamers', went Top 10 and Top 20 respectively. A seasonal standalone single, 'December Will Be Magic Again', fared less well at the end of the year, only just entering the Top 30. Nevertheless, she was voted 'Best female artist of 1980' in *Melody Maker* and *Sounds* end-of-year readers' polls.

Her next single in the summer of 1981, 'Sat in Your Lap', preceded its parent album by over a year. *The Dreaming*, released in September 1982, and the first that she had produced herself, was greeted with a mixed critical reception, some baffled by the dense soundscapes she had created with extensive use of the Fairlight CMI and the largely more experimental, less commercial songs. It reached No. 3, but sales were disappointing, while of the next two singles, the title track only just reached the Top 50 and 'There Goes a Tenner' merely scraped into the Top 100.

Keen to establish a greater degree of independence and not have to rely on the expense of using EMI studios, she took advantage of a break from recording by creating her own studio where she could work in her own time. After a three-year hiatus, she returned in August 1985 with the first fruits of her forty-eight-track home studio. 'Running Up That Hill' became her second most successful single ever in Britain and her American breakthrough, reaching No. 30 on the Billboard charts. The album *Hounds of Love*, released a month later and acclaimed at once as a dazzling return to form, topped the album charts for four weeks and spawned a further three singles, all reaching the Top 40.

At the behest of EMI, Kate's next project was a retrospective, *The Whole Story*, released in November 1986 and preceded two weeks earlier by a new single, 'Experiment IV'. For the album, she had re-recorded the lead vocal for 'Wuthering Heights' to bring the song more in line with her newly matured voice, and she later admitted she would have liked to have done the same with other early recordings done when in her teens. She was enjoying a high profile at the time, also duetting with Peter Gabriel on the Top 10 hit 'Don't Give Up', and winning the Best Brit Artist award at the annual BRIT Awards in London. In the spring of 1987, she was one of several contemporary singers to contribute a couple of lines to a No. 1 charity single, a new recording of The Beatles' 'Let It Be', credited to Ferry Aid with all monies raised going to the Zeebrugge Disaster Fund, launched after the ferry *Herald of Free Enterprise* capsized in March 1987 after leaving Zeebrugge, resulting in the deaths of 193 passengers and crew. As a guest vocalist, between 1980 and 1996, she appeared on albums by Roy Harper, Big Country, Midge Ure, Go West, Alan Stivell, and Prince.

Now more in control of her career than ever, new albums were following at an ever slower rate than before. 'The Sensual World' was released in October 1989, reaching No. 2 in Britain, and receiving major promotion in America, where she had just signed with Columbia Records for future releases. For the previous four years or so, she had, however, been able to exert more control over her appearances in the media at home and abroad. The image of her as an enthusiastic, idealistic girl not yet out of her teens still lingered, and it was no surprise that she sometimes resented the constant merry-go-round of interviews each time an album came out, often on light entertainment TV shows with either ill-informed or downright patronising presenters. Having proved herself as an artist of some worth and not a nine-day wonder pop puppet, she would now call the shots. As Maddy Prior of Steeleye Span later acknowledged, Kate was the first one who said, 'I'm going to write [the next album] for a year, record it for a year, sell it for a year.'[4]

The Red Shoes, released in 1993, was inspired by the 1948 film by Michael Powell and Emeric Pressburger. It was dedicated to the memory of her mother, Hannah, who had died the previous year, and debuted in the American Top 30, the first time one of her albums had ever charted that high. She made a rare personal appearance in America that December, signing autographs at Tower Records on the Lower East Side, New York. The resulting line of admirers stretched almost six blocks and required her to extend her appearance by several hours. Less successful was a short musical film, *The Line, the Cross and the Curve*, which she directed as well as starred in alongside Miranda Richardson and her early dance and mime mentor Lindsay Kemp. It was basically an extended music video comprising songs from the last album, and received a limited cinema release prior to being made available on video. In later years, she admitted that it had been a failure, dismissing it as 'a load of bollocks'.

Twelve years elapsed before her next release (to put that into perspective, The Beatles' entire career, from signing to EMI to releasing their last album *Let It Be*, lasted just eight). During the break from her musical career, she and her husband, Danny McIntosh, became parents when Albert ('Bertie') was born in 1998. Speculation had long abounded as to whether there would ever be another new album or not. Though she was adamant that it never happened, she was much amused by an apocryphal story that some excited EMI executives, or perhaps only the CEO, Tony Wadsworth, came to visit her at home after she had invited him to show off her latest creation, because it was turning out so well. Instead of playing him demos of her new songs, she produced some cakes that she had just baked in the oven.

Everyone's patience was rewarded in 2005 when the double album/CD *Aerial* was released. Another six-year silence followed before the appearance of *Director's Cut* in 2011, a collection of eleven redone songs taken from *The Sensual World* and *The Red Shoes*. She claimed she had never been quite satisfied with what was released, and decided to rework elements in the chosen numbers, recutting all vocals and drums, and leaving virtually everything else unchanged. Later that year, she also released a new collection, *50 Words for Snow*. Both records appeared on her newly-formed own label, Fish People, thus named as she 'thought it was a bit of fun, rather than a very lofty or serious name'.[5]

In the New Year's Honours of 2013, she was awarded the CBE (Commander of the Order of the British Empire) for services to British music. During March the following year, she announced her forthcoming return to the stage for the first time in thirty-five years, to perform a series of concerts under the name 'Before the Dawn', at London's Hammersmith Apollo Theatre from August to October. Fifteen shows were initially booked and sold out within minutes of going on sale, as were another seven nights scheduled immediately afterwards. Like the 'Tour of Life', they comprised an ambitious blend of music, dance, and drama, with a set list that excluded material from the first four albums and focused on songs from *Hounds of Love* onwards, the concerts received enthusiastic reviews, and received the Editor's Award at the London Theatre Awards. Recordings of the performances resulted in a live album, also called *Before the Dawn*, in November 2016, as well as a new chart record. In one week in August 2014, she had become the first female singer to have eleven albums, comprising what was at the time her complete back catalogue, in the Top 50 album chart at once.

Thereafter, she embarked on a comprehensive programme of remastering her back catalogue. In November 2018, a series of boxed sets appeared, two on CD and four on vinyl. The second CD set included four bonus discs featuring rare and unreleased material, including demos, 12-inch mixes, alternate versions, and interpretations of other artists' songs. The four rarities discs received a stand-alone release in March 2019 as *Other Sides*.

As a person, Kate Bush has always strongly defended her privacy. Over the years, several journalists found her polite but guarded, ready to please but rarely comfortable with being interviewed, reluctant to be drawn at length, accepting such encounters as a necessary evil to be endured, and a tiresome distraction from the business of practising and perfecting her craft. Like some authors who increasingly preferred to shun the limelight as their careers progressed, she seemed content to release her material to the public and let it speak for itself. One writer, Simon Reynolds, managed to elicit a comment from her about how she saw her art, a curiously enigmatic manifesto that was at once elusive yet honest:

> That's what all art's about—a sense of moving away from boundaries that you can't—in real-life. Like a dancer is always trying to fly, really—to do something that's just not possible. But you try to do as much as you can within those physical boundaries. All art is like that: a form of exploration, of making up stories. Writing, film, sculpture, music: it's all make-believe, really.[6]

When the first single and album were released, her songs sounded utterly unlike anything else in the mainstream pop and rock market. Like David

Bowie and very few others, she was impossible to pigeonhole in a single musical genre, be it pop, electropop, folk rock, art rock, or progressive rock, and her imaginative dramatic lyrical gifts put her in another class entirely. The continuing quality of her subsequent work proved that she was no flash-in-the-pan. Moreover, she was one of the first artists to exploit the music video as a medium, a process that became increasingly important as a promotional tool for artists worldwide with the arrival of MTV in 1981.

Like any successful artist, she has always had her detractors and critics seemingly unmoved by her work. Reviewing one of her 1979 shows in *New Musical Express*, Charles Shaar Murray dismissed her performance as a throwback to 'all the unpleasant aspects of David Bowie in the Mainman era [the early 1970s]'. Radio 1's John Peel was similarly unimpressed, saying he could never take her seriously because of her voice. They were firmly in a minority. Others in the media, and indeed her own peers, have admired her for her strikingly unusual, literate, and complex songs with their breadth of subject matter as well as her command of the concert stage, Annie Lennox, Elton John, Midge Ure, Prince, Brett Anderson of Suede, Björk, Beverley Craven, Stevie Nicks, P. J. Harvey, Tori Amos, Alison Goldfrapp, and Coldplay all unreservedly praised her and in some cases cited her as a major influence. John Lydon, formerly Johnny Rotten of The Sex Pistols, was also a fervent admirer, describing her work as 'beauty beyond belief', and even writing a song for her, 'Bird in Hand', about the exploitation of parrots. She reciprocated her admiration of his art, though it did not extend to accepting and recording the number.

By music business standards, hers has been an unconventional career. In terms of regular shows or tours, she was absent from the stage for over thirty years, and at one stage kept her fans waiting twelve years for the next album, a time in which she and her family succeeded in keeping well away from the public eye. The subject matter of her songs was frequently unusual, questioning, and worlds away from the often limited lyrical preoccupations of her contemporaries. When journalists Ed Power and Roisin O'Connor chose their forty favourite song lyrics of all time, Kate's 'Cloudbusting' was high on the list. 'Few artists use surrealism as successfully as Kate Bush – or draw inspiration from such unusual places,' they opined.[7] In recent years, as she has become less prolific, she has given fewer interviews and therefore not explained the inspiration or meaning behind her newer songs, leaving it for the listener to decide. There are several online forums in which fans have readily advanced their own theories, on which I have drawn from time to time.

Her song structures have often deviated from the normal template of verse/chorus times two or three, bridge, back to verse/chorus, or similar, and generally eschewing conventional rhyming patterns. 'They're not normal songs,' Elton John said in 2014. 'None of her songs have been normal ... she's just unique, she's a mystery.'[8] Maybe it is significant that the vast majority of cover versions from her catalogue have been by groups and artists from a younger generation of alternative music acts, as opposed to the older mainstream guard. Her videos were likewise as innovative as her striking early stage shows. Once established, she did everything at her own pace, sometimes in direct contravention to what an often bemused record company wished her to do. In the process, over four decades has she enjoyed a consistent level of success, critical respect, and loyalty from a fan base that few other songwriters could ever dream about.

The Kick Inside

UK: Released 17 February 1978, EMI, No 6 (2014 reissue, No 24)
US: Released 1978, EMI America
Personnel: Kate Bush: lead and backing vocals, piano
          Andrew Powell: arrangements, keyboards (2), piano, Fender Rhodes
          (3), bass guitar, celeste (6), synthesizer (9), beer bottles (12)
          Duncan Mackay: piano, Fender Rhodes (1, 10), synthesizer (3),
          Hammond organ (4, 6, 7), clavinet (4)
          Ian Bairnson: electric guitar, acoustic guitar (except 2), backing
          vocals (9), beer bottles (12)
          David Paton: bass guitar (1, 3, 4, 7, 9-12), acoustic guitar (6, 9),
          backing vocals (9)
          Stuart Elliott: drums (1, 3-4, 7-12), percussion (9, 12)
          Alan Skidmore: tenor saxophone (2)
          Paul Keogh: electric guitar, acoustic guitar (2)
          Alan Parker: acoustic guitar (2)
          Bruce Lynch: bass guitar (2)
          Barry de Souza: drums (2)
          Morris Pert: percussion (3, 4, 6), boobam (12)
          Paddy Bush: mandolin (9), backing vocals (11)
          David Katz: orchestral contractor (1-3, 5, 6, 9-11, 13)
Recorded at AIR Studios, London, July–August 1977, except 2 and 5
Produced by Andrew Powell

Kate's first album began as a series of demo tapes, paid for by Dave Gilmour
of Pink Floyd. After he played them to executives at EMI, she was signed to
the label. Two of the demos, 'The Man With the Child in His Eyes' and 'The
Saxophone Song', recorded in June 1975, were included on the album, and
the remaining eleven tracks were recorded within six weeks, two summers
later. The KT Bush Band had been playing live in London pubs shortly before

the recordings took place and she wanted to use them on the album, but EMI insisted that she had to use experienced musicians instead. The core of the studio group consisted of Ian Bairnson and David Paton from Pilot, and Duncan Mackay and Stuart Elliott from Steve Harley and Cockney Rebel, with whom Powell had worked previously.

The thirteen songs chosen were just the tip of the iceberg, for when Kate and Andrew Powell, her producer, originally sat down to plan the project, she had around 120 from which to draw up a shortlist. She had been well prepared for the occasion, and worked out the songs in precise detail before they entered the studio. Having a clear idea of how the final work should sound, she did not improvise or alter a single lyric. Jon Kelly, the engineer, was very impressed with how self-assured and professional she was despite her youth and lack of experience. At once, from the moment she walked into the control room, he could tell that she wanted to be there, in full command of the record she was about to make. She was remarkably astute, and at the same time very easy to work with.

Musically and lyrically, the songs were startling. Were they middle-of-the-road fare with a few unsettling edges, or progressive rock numbers with themes encompassing everything from the environment and literary villains to forbidden sexual passion and Russian mystics? Some of the session men were just as puzzled by the music as listeners and critics would be by the time it was released. Not for some years did it dawn on most people that, at a time when punk was doing its best to turn the music world upside down, here was a new singer-songwriter who 'appeared the very epitome of a nice, middle-class girl, and her music, while odder than the usual bubblegum pop, had none of the sharp edges, urgency or bumptiousness associated with punk. In retrospect, however, she represents a much deeper revolution than that genre's superficial antipathy ... for in her work can be registered the subtler, but more potent, liberating power of imagination and art'. Unsuspecting parents, purchasing the album for their son or daughter who had been bewitched by its chart-topping single, were almost certainly unaware that they were buying a record containing lyrics dealing with such taboos as sex, 'that time of the month', and even incest.[1] It might not have worn the badge of anarchy on its sleeve, but beneath the sophisticated, harmless veneer, surprise lurked just beneath the surface.

By any standards, the record was a startling achievement, and not just because it was the debut album by an artist recorded around the time of her nineteenth birthday. In the words of her biographer Graeme Thomson, despite her desire to 'masculinise' her muse, it remains one of the most profoundly female albums ever made.[2]

Tracks

1. 'Moving' 3.01

Track one on the debut album, 'about how a person discovers free expression', was written as a tribute to Lindsay Kemp, the dancer and choreographer with whom Kate had studied mime since soon after leaving school, and who she said 'opened up [her] eyes to the meanings of movement'. A few years earlier, he had also worked with David Bowie in a similar capacity. Returning home one day, he was startled to find a copy of *The Kick Inside* under his door and learn that the song had been dedicated to him. Having always found her so shy, at least until he was able to bring her 'out of her shell', he was also amazed to learn that she was a singer—and now clearly a professional one at that.

It was also inspired by whales, whom she found had a common factor with her studies of dance in that they shared a similar grace. At her request, as a gentle introduction for the listener, the track begins and ends with sounds of a whale song sampled from *Songs of the Humpback Whale*, an LP including recordings made by Dr Roger S. Payne, released in 1970 after Judy Collins had sampled it for her rendition of *Farewell Tarwathe*. It soon became the bestselling environmental album of all time. Some may find the first few seconds rather chilling, but taking on a warmer quality once Kate begins to sing.

The track was only released as a single in Japan, with 'Wuthering Heights' on the B-side. In the UK and most other countries, it became the B-side to 'The Man with the Child in His Eyes'.

2. 'The Saxophone Song' 3.51

The first of two songs from the AIR sessions recorded in the summer of 1975 as a demo and produced by David Gilmour, it was also one of her earliest, written when she was about fifteen. Despite theories that it was meant to be about David Bowie, whose farewell live show as Ziggy Stardust she attended in 1973, she insisted it was purely about the instrument. 'I love saxophones so I wanted to write a song about them,' she said. 'I think of a beautiful sax like a human being, a sensuous shining man being taken over by the instrument. The perfect setting was this smokey bar in Berlin with nobody listening except me in a corner.'[3] Keyboards and sturdy drum patterns drive the song effortlessly until a beautifully fluid, jazzy sax enters stage left about one minute in.

Its only release as a single was as a postcard single in Poland.

3. 'Strange Phenomena' 2.57

This was inspired by the coincidences that happen to people on a regular basis. We can probably all recall instances, Kate said, when we have been thinking about a particular individual and then meet a mutual friend who without being prompted will start talking about that person. 'That's a very basic way of explaining what I mean, but these "clusters of coincidence" occur all the time. We are surrounded by strange phenomena, but very few people are aware of it. Most take it as being part of everyday life.'[4] One reference in the first verse—'every girl knows about the punctual blues'—is certainly part of a woman's everyday life. Musically, a twinkling piano intro makes way for a richer, stately arrangement in which synthesiser and strings enter, all underpinned by the restrained rhythm section, reverting in the last twenty seconds or so to the same piano sound that introduced the song.

It was released as a single in Brazil only on a four-track EP, *4 Succesos*, in 1979 with three tracks from the second album.

4. 'Kite' 2.56

Reggae-style lead and bass guitar emphasise the flavour of a number that was, to quote its creator, 'written like a Bob Marley song'. Lyrically, it is a paean to independence and freedom. Kate explained that the central character starts to feel he is rooted to the ground, while an invisible force is pulling him up into the sky. A voice is calling him to 'Come up and be a kite,' as he is drawn up to the sky and takes the form and texture of one. Next he is flying 'like a feather on the wind', and enjoys the sensation at first, until a longing for home and the security of the ground take over.

It was issued as the B-side of 'Wuthering Heights' in the UK and most overseas territories.

5. 'The Man with the Child in His Eyes' 2.39

Another of Kate's earliest compositions, written when she was thirteen, this was the other recording from the 1975 demo sessions that sounded good enough to use on the album. It featured her on the piano, without bass or drums, but instead accompanied by a string section from the London Symphony Orchestra conducted by David Katz, a prospect that she later admitted 'terrified' her at the time.

The album version opens with the first verse. When it became the second single, with the addition at the beginning of a spoken 'He's here—he's here', and a chuckle, it reached No. 6 in Britain in the summer of 1978. Six months later, it appeared as a single in America, becoming her first hit on the Billboard singles chart at No. 85. In 1979, it won the Ivor Novello Award for Outstanding British Lyric.

When talking about the song at the time, Kate said it was about her theory that she had observed in most of the men that she knew, basically the fact that that they were 'just little boys inside' and remained thus throughout life, yet still managed to retain a certain magic. She saw it as a very natural, basic instinct that women looked continually for their father throughout their lives, as did men continually look for their mother in the women that they met: 'You look for that security that the opposite sex in your parenthood gave you as a child'.[5]

The inspiration for the song went rather deeper than that—back to her relationship with her first serious boyfriend, Steve Blacknell, a future TV and radio presenter. Some thirty years later, after putting the original sheet of handwritten lyrics she had given him at the time up for sale online with an asking price of £10,000, he told the press the full story of how she had been 'his first true love'. At the time, he was working as a cleaner in a local hospital, and planning a career in the music industry. Even then, he said, she had her heart set on becoming a global star, he was going to be a flash DJ, and one day he would introduce her on *Top of the Pops*. In the summer of 1975, he got his break and landed a job as a marketing assistant with Decca Records. It was only then, he later recalled, that he finally came to hear her music—and it was a day he would never forget: 'I went round to her house and she led me to the room where the piano was. I thought "Oh my God." What I heard made my soul stand on end. I realised there and then that I was in love with a genius'. They later drifted apart, but he had the word of those close to her that the song had been inspired by him, 'and I know that those words were given to me by someone very special.'[6]

The song has attracted a number of cover versions, including those by Natalie Cole and Charlotte Church. Dusty Springfield and Steve Hogarth of Marillion, as a solo artist, also performed it on stage.

6. *'Wuthering Heights'* 4.28

The song that made Kate a household name was one of the last to be written for the album. In the early months of 1977, she was rehearsing and playing with The KT Bush Band and had not had time to write any new material for a while. Shortly before sessions for the album were due to begin, the muse revisited her late one night as she was sitting at her piano looking through the open curtains at a full moon. She had just watched a 1967 BBC dramatisation—or at least part of it, perhaps only the closing scenes, according to some sources—of Emily Brontë's 1847 novel. After writing the song, she read the book and discovered that she and the author had the same birthday, 30 July. There was a further coincidence (more 'strange phenomena'?) in that, like Earnshaw, she was once known in the family as Cathy—as a child—before she decided to change it to Kate.

The story, the setting, the surreal vision of a hand reaching through the window, and above all the character of the heroine, or female villain, added up to a combination that fascinated her at once. 'This young girl in an era when the female role was so inferior,' she said, 'and she was coming out with this passionate, heavy stuff. Great subject matter for a song.'[7] In three succinct minutes, the lyrics tell of the situation at the end of the film from the perspective of Cathy, 'a really vile person ... so headstrong'. Once she has died, her spirit comes back across 'the wiley, windy moors' to come and get Heathcliff again. She needs to possess him, 'I hated you, I loved you too', and entreats him, 'I've come home, I'm so cold, Let me in through your window!' To Kate, it was a sterling example of somebody, albeit a fictional character, who was obsessive enough to go to extremes to get what they wanted, and 'wouldn't even be alone when she was dead'.

When she visited Andrew Powell at his home, and sat down at his piano to play and sing the song, he immediately recognised it as something 'really extraordinary,' and agreed they should definitely record it.

Jon Kelly, the engineer, recalled Kate's recording of the song. She was imitating a witch, a mad lady from the Yorkshire Moors, and was very theatrical about it all: 'She was such a mesmerising performer, she threw her heart and soul into everything she did that it was difficult to ever fault her or say, "You could do better"'.[8]

Because of the subject matter, Kate knew instinctively that she needed to sing in 'a high-pitched wailing voice', an astonishing vocal that the average casual pop radio listener would find an acquired taste. When recording the vocal, she deliberately entered into the spirit of the song, projecting herself into the role of her character. As Cathy was a spirit, 'it needed some kind of ethereal effect, and it seemed to be the best way to do it, to get a high register'.

Ian Bairnson called the song 'a great track [in] a style which flew in the face of everything else which was round at the time. We kept looking at each other thinking, "This is so different but interesting—it will either do really well, or bomb."'[9] When he came to set up his guitar and play the solo, he got a note to feed back to the amplifier. As they realised it was exactly the same note on which Kate ended her vocal, Kelly shouted at him to keep going and he would fade him in. While she was singing the last note, Bairnson was faded in holding that same note and he launched into the solo—'entirely seat-of-the-pants stuff!'[10]

Bob Mercer, the general manager at EMI, originally chose 'James and the Cold Gun' as the lead single, but she was determined to use 'Wuthering Heights' instead. Although she may not have believed that it was her most commercial offering, to her it was far more representative of her work, much more unusual, had a very English storyline, and she was 'into reaching far more than the ordinary market'.[11] She firmly disputed the later assertion that she burst into tears while imploring him to change his mind, but she undoubtedly put her foot down and he was persuaded. To her, it had to be the single: 'I had to fight off a few other people's opinions but in the end they agreed with me'. He told her that it was of no consequence or importance to him what the first single was, as he did not think she was a singles act but an albums act and he thought 'it could take at least three albums for us to gain any traction at all.' In what with hindsight seems an astonishing (or as Kate might have said, 'amazing') admission, he confessed he would not have minded if someone had suggested they never put a single out from the LP at all.[12] While there had in the past been exceptions to every rule (such as Mike Oldfield's *Tubular Bells* five years earlier, or Led Zeppelin's entire career), conventional music business wisdom and marketing both suggested that by the late 1970s the best launchpad for a hit album, particularly by a new artist, was a major hit single. Had 'Wuthering Heights' not been such a soaraway success, it was unlikely that 'The Kick Inside' would ever have enjoyed more than modest sales, or that Kate's career would have taken off into the stratosphere so quickly.

Plans were made for the 45 to be released on 4 November 1977. Kate was not satisfied with the picture on the sleeve and insisted it had to be replaced. EMI agreed, having had second thoughts for a different reason, the likelihood that it would be overwhelmed in the Christmas market and would have more impact if they delayed it until the new year (one week later, the same company was to issue Wings' 'Mull of Kintyre', which would top the charts over the festive season and stay in pole position for nine weeks, becoming the best-selling single in British music history to date). Some advance promotional copies had already been sent out to journalists and radio stations, and EMI followed it with letters asking the latter not to play it yet. Most obliged, apart from Tony Myatt, a Capital Radio presenter. He and his producer loved it, continued to air it regularly, and listeners were ringing up to ask who was on this record that they could not find to buy anywhere.

Released on 20 January 1978, it found a ready champion on Radio 1 in David 'Kid' Jensen, and once added to the station's playlist entered the Top 50 three weeks later at No. 42, then rose to No. 27. That same week, she made her first appearance on *Top of the Pops*. As the ultimate perfectionist, she found the experience an absolute nightmare as she was not allowed to provide her own band, the producer Robin Nash telling her that as a solo artist, Musicians' Union rules dictated that she had to perform with a backing track hastily recorded by the BBC resident orchestra. Seeing the result on TV later, she said, was like watching herself die.

The record reached No. 1 in March, and stayed there for four weeks, the first occasion a female singer had topped the British charts with a self-penned song. It was also No. 1 in Ireland, Italy, Australia, and New Zealand, reached the Top 10 in Belgium, the Netherlands, Finland, Norway, Sweden, and Switzerland, and the Top 20 in Austria and West Germany.

Critic Simon Reynolds called it 'Gothic romance distilled into four-and-a-half minutes of gaseous rhapsody'.[13] John Lydon remarked that when he first heard it, he thought it 'extremely challenging, the vocal—it was almost hysterical, and it was so up there, the register, but it was absolutely fascinating. And I know at the time a lot of my friends couldn't bear it, they thought it was just too much—but that's exactly what drew me in'.[14] Some initially saw it as a weird semi-novelty hit from a new singer surely destined for the one-hit wonder hall of fame. A few members of the Brontë Society hated it, called it 'a disgrace', and claimed it cheapened an important literary work. Kate took it in her stride, pointing out that many people had been drawn to reading and enjoying the book after hearing the song. The novel was on the GCE English Literature syllabus that year, and she was delighted when many a student went on record as saying how the song had helped them. Alan Bentley, appointed director of the Brontë Parsonage Museum in Haworth in 2001, readily admitted that one of the main factors that brought people there from all over the world was the Kate Bush connection, and 'people often arrive at the novels' as a result of the song.

The Society's early disdain was soon forgotten. Forty years later, Kate was one of four notable women invited to pay tribute to the Brontë sisters, the others being poets Carol Ann Duffy (Poet Laureate), Jackie Kay, and novelist Jeanette Winterson. Each was asked to provide words for a permanent art installation on the Yorkshire moors that had inspired their writing, by writing a short piece of poetry or prose to be engraved on stones positioned over the 8-mile route between the sisters' birthplace in Thornton and the family home, the Haworth parsonage. Kate's contribution was a ten-line poem, in tribute to Emily.[15]

Like many British performers from the mid-1970s onwards, Kate readily acknowledged David Bowie as one of her foremost influences, once saying that 'Starman' was her 'bolt out of the blue' musical experience. It has also been suggested that Ian Bairnson's powerful guitar solo on 'Wuthering Heights' closely mirrors Mick Ronson's playing on 'Starman', to say nothing of the coincidence that Stuart Elliott had been a member of Cockney Rebel, who were seen as one of the more art rock-inspired glam acts alongside Bowie and Roxy Music: 'So think of "Wuthering Heights" as a post-glam rococo masterpiece, a one-off diamond in 1978's rough'.[16]

Eight years later, Kate re-recorded the song with a new vocal track (see p. xx).

Several other acts have also issued their own versions. The best-known, in America at least, is that on Pat Benatar's second album, *Crimes of Passion*, released in 1980 and selling over 4 million copies in her home territory. As one of the few non-original songs on the album, it helped to introduce Kate to an American audience as a songwriter while her own recorded work was still almost unknown.

7. *'James and the Cold Gun'* 3.34

There are at least two or three different theories as to the inspiration for this song. Some suggest it was James Bond, Ian Fleming's legendary hero, while some ascribe it to *The Day of the Jackal*, Frederick Forsyth's thriller about the would-be assassin of President Charles de Gaulle of France, later a film starring

Edward Fox. Others point to one of the leaders of the James-Younger Gang, a band of Wild West American outlaws in the nineteenth century, perhaps the notorious Jesse James himself. According to Kate, it was about nobody in particular. When she wrote the song, James seemed the right name. It was therefore the tale of a totally fictitious outlaw who had gone on the run and hit the bottle, while the rest of the gang missed him and wanted him to come back. So did his lady Jeannie, from the casino, 'still a-waiting in her big brass bed'—a recurring motif in rock music since being used by Bob Dylan in 'Lay Lady Lay'.

It is easy to see why EMI wanted this as the first single, as on initial listen it sounds far and away the most commercial track. For Bob Mercer, it was 'a cleverer song and more accessible' than 'Wuthering Heights'. It had been one of the highlights of Kate's repertoire with The KT Bush Band, with a little help from a dry ice machine, Kate's swift costume change into a Western cowgirl dress, and a fake gun with which she would pretend to shoot people (in an age when such theatrical props would raise scarcely an eyebrow). With its bouncy rhythm and snappy piano chords introduction followed by predominant rock guitar, bubbling organ, and some spirited work on the drums, instrumentally at least, it sounds closer to Suzi Quatro territory, certainly until the boogie gives way to a slower more stately section that takes up the last sixty seconds until it fades out. Ian Bairnson was proud of the guitar solo he contributed, but because of the playing time restrictions of a vinyl album, it had to be severely edited.

An in-concert version on *Live at Hammersmith Odeon*, recorded in 1979 and released on home video two years later, and as part of a boxed set with a CD in 1994, ended with a guitar solo played jointly by Brian Bath and Alan Murphy, lasting almost five minutes—longer than the vocal section preceding it. With a running time of eight minutes and forty-four seconds, it was by far the longest of the twelve tracks featured. Bairnson's hopes that the full studio track may eventually appear on a remixed and remastered CD version of the album remain as yet unrealised. Somewhere in the vaults, perhaps, languishes a two-part epic that could just be Kate's own version of Derek and the Dominos' 'Layla'.

8. *'Feel It'* 3.02

The only song on the album accompanied by Kate on the piano without any other instrumentation, it is probably the most erotically-charged, being the tender tale of a young woman's first intimate encounter: 'Here comes one and one makes one/The glorious union, well, it could be love/Or it could be just lust but it will be fun'. It all takes place after a party as she is invited back to the man's parlour, and the picture is built up—a little nervous laughter as they lock the door, and her stockings fall to the floor. Every detail is carefully built up as the woman seductively surrenders herself in a remarkably delicate, tasteful number, all the better for its sheer musical simplicity.

9. 'Oh to Be in Love' 3.18

A song first recorded as a demo in the summer of 1976, this continues the theme of the previous track. Once again, the lyric is charmingly simple, with its chorus message of 'Oh, to be in love—and never to get out again'. It is all about the joy, the rapture of that blissful state when 'all the colours look brighter now' and wishing to freeze that treasured moment in time, or to 'Stop the swing of the pendulum'.

The backing is a little more ornate, with restrained drums, bass, and the sound of male backing vocals, which it has been suggested might be meant to evoke Roman Catholic liturgical chanting—a throwback to Kate's convent school days. This was the only song from the album that was not performed on the Tour of Life show in 1978.

10. 'L'Amour Looks Something Like You' 2.27

The third song in a row about passion, this examines the agony of unfulfilled love, even frustration, through the eyes of a woman. The scene is all set as her lover comes out of the night, 'wearing a mask in white colour', as her eyes are shining on the wine. They move into the boudoir together—and then the morning comes. She is hanging on the old goose moon, which could be either the full moon or else the time from late March to late April when the Canada goose returns from the south. Her lover looks like an angel, 'sleeping it off at a station—were you only passing through? I'm dying for you just to touch me'. The tenderness is matched by the simplicity of the backing, just subtle touches on the drums, lead, and bass guitars.

11. 'Them Heavy People' 3.04

The idea for this song came to Kate one day when she was sitting in her parents' house. It all started from the phrase 'rolling the ball', which sent her straight to the piano. Basically about religion and the teachings of Jesus and Gurdjieff, a Russian mystic and philosopher who was a regular subject of conversation in the Bush household, both of whom are mentioned by name, it expresses a yearning to learn as much as possible, while she is still young. Teachers are ready to help her, now that she realises that 'every one of us has a heaven inside', opening doorways 'that I thought were shut for good'. She once said that it was like a prayer, 'and it reminds me of direction'.

Musically most of the song is mid-tempo, with the guitar and rhythm section adding a subtle hint of reggae, though less transparently than 'Kite'. One of the more obviously commercial tracks on the album, it was suggested by the record company at one point as the second single, until she insisted on 'The Man with the Child in His Eyes'. She was never completely satisfied with the recorded version, feeling it should have been much looser.

A live version from the tour subsequently became the opening track on the *On Stage* four-track EP, reaching No. 10 in the British chart in September

1979. The record was issued as an EP playing at 33 rpm and also as a 45 rpm double single for the media, the other three tracks being 'Don't Push Your Foot on the Heartbrake', 'James and the Cold Gun', and 'L'Amour Looks Something Like You'. In Japan, it was issued as a single in its own right, where the picture sleeve shows the Japanese title as a translation of 'Rolling the Ball'.

12. 'Room for the Life' 4.03
To a very restrained backing of piano, the rhythm section and subtle guitar, this gentle song about the female of the species was Kate's expression of belief that as women are mentally and physically programmed to bear children, the female of the species possesses a much greater instinct of survival and protection, and they should therefore use their advantage to help them rather than play games with them.

When interviewed a couple of years later, she said many people had misconstrued it as a feminist number, something she found slightly disappointing. Her actual message was that women should 'go a bit easier on men because we are the ones with survival inside us, we carry the next generation, we have the will to keep going, we keep bouncing back'. Femininity, she insisted, was not particularly strong in her songs. She had always felt there was something lacking in her feminine role, and it was not a major theme in her songs. 'Being brought up with two brothers I'd sit philosophising with them while my girlfriends wanted to talk about clothes and food. Maybe it's the male energy to be the hunter and I feel I have that in me'.[17]

13. 'The Kick Inside' 3.30
Murder ballads had long been part of the British folk tradition, but with a few exceptions (major hits by Tom Jones and The Bee Gees in 1968, to name but two) never really had a place in mainstream pop. The title track of Kate's debut album took its inspiration from an old English-Scottish song, 'Lucy Wan', one of many included in Ralph Vaughan Williams and A. L. Lloyd's *Penguin Book of English Folk Songs*, and later recorded by Martin Carthy and Dave Swarbrick. In the traditional version, Lucy admits to her brother that she is carrying his child, whereupon he cuts her head off with his sword, confesses all to his mother, and tells her that he intends to sail away to a distant land and will never return. Kate's rewriting of the story retains the brother-sister incest element, but she sends him the news in a suicide note. She is taking her own life in order to preserve his good name and that of the family. The song itself is the note, and by the time he reads it, she will be gone: 'The kicking here inside makes me leave you behind … you must lose me like an arrow shot into the killer storm'.

Julie Covington, a long-time friend of the family for some years, recorded a cover version on her eponymous album released later that year.

Lionheart

UK: Released 12 November 1978, EMI, No. 6
US: Released 1984, EMI America
Personnel: Kate Bush: vocals, harmony vocals, piano
Andrew Powell: arrangements, Joanna strumentum (8), harmonium (10)
Duncan Mackay: Fender Rhodes (1, 2, 4), synthesiser (3, 9, 10)
Francis Monkman: harpsichord (4, 5), Hammond organ (6)
Richard Harvey: recorders (5)
Ian Bairnson: electric guitar (1–4, 6, 10), acoustic guitar (2, 10), rhythm guitar (9)
Paddy Bush: mandolin (3), harmony vocals (4, 5, 8), slide guitar (4), strumento de porco (psaltery), mandocello and pan flute (8)
Brian Bath: guitars (3)
David Paton: bass guitar (1, 2, 4, 6, 9)
Del Palmer: bass guitar (3, 8, 10)
Stuart Elliott: drums (1, 2, 4, 6, 9, 10), percussion (1, 8, 9)
Charlie Morgan: drums (3, 8)
David Katz: orchestral contractor (9, 10)
Recorded at Super Bear Studios, Berre-les-Alpes, France, July-September 1978
Produced by Andrew Powell, assisted by Kate Bush

The success of *The Kick Inside* had exceeded all expectations, and EMI saw no reason to alter a winning formula. Plans for a tour of Britain were briefly discussed, but Kate wanted to focus on making more records first, and the label were eager for a second album. Most of the songs chosen were from the large collection she had written before the start of her recording career, with 'Symphony in Blue', 'Full House', and 'Coffee Homeground' being the only recent compositions used. In between a hectic schedule of promotional duties at home and overseas, she and the KT Bush Band—Brian Bath, Del Palmer, and Charlie Morgan, who had replaced Vic King on drums—recorded some demos, with guitarist Brian Bath working as musical director. For Del Palmer, it would be the beginning of a very long association with Kate. They had a personal relationship for some years, and after that ran its course, on this and every subsequent album, he played bass guitar and/or engineered.

That summer, she was booked to go and work in Superbear Studios, Berre-Les-Alpes, near Nice in south-east France. It would be the only time she recorded outside Britain. Once again, she asked if she could use her own band, but Powell saw no reason to depart from calling on the same tried and trusted team as before. As she insisted, he agreed to compromise with a combination of the two. After a few days, he considered that Kate's band lacked studio experience and, while they may have worked well as a unit playing live, failed to adapt quickly to the very different studio environment. He had his way in the end, with 'her' musicians, the KT Bush Band, and also her brother, Paddy, on several different instruments having very limited input. The producer conceded that 'some of the tracks they did rather well, others just didn't work', so they had to be redone with the players that he had recruited or used on the first album.[1] As Ian Bairnson conceded, it was a difficult situation for all of them, but it was not so much 'looking at keeping your friends happy [as making] the best possible record'.[2] They returned to London in September for strings and additional overdubs to be added, and it was mixed in October for release the following month, with 'Hammer Horror' preceding it as the first single.

Kate thought the album could have been so much better, made too quickly and under too much pressure, and she was determined that in future she would work at her own pace. 'Considering how quickly we made it it's a bloody good album, but I'm not really happy with it,' she commented eleven years later.[3] In America, it was not released until 1984, following the success of her fourth album *The Dreaming*. Years later, one reviewer wrote with hindsight that it was 'bursting with ideas that were not quite fully formed'.

Two songs proved a gift to comedians on television. Impressionist Faith Brown's parody of 'Wow' on *The Faith Brown Chat Show* featured her dancing routine being cut short when she was whisked away by an invisible harness, while the title track was spoofed as 'Oh England My Leotard' by Pamela Stephenson on *Not the Nine O'Clock News* in a song set to the tune of 'Them Heavy People' ('Went to Cairo and I read the Gnostic, Apocryphon of John in the original Coptic ... Studied acupuncture and the Bible ... They only buy my latest hits because they like my latex tits').

Tracks

1. 'Symphony in Blue' 3.35

One of three songs newly written for the album earlier that year (the others being 'Full House' and 'Coffee Homeground'), the lyric is Kate's attempt at describing her own beliefs in a fairly abstract way, as would be the case with one of her later songs, 'Cloudbusting' (see pp. 61–2). Her descriptions of God ('Go blowing my mind on God, the light in the dark'), the colour blue ('The colour of my room and my mood'), and sex ('The more I think about sex, the better it gets'), owed something to her having read Peter Reich's *A Book of Dreams*, a memoir of his father Wilhelm, an Austrian psychoanalyst. Her lyric ends with a gentle pun: 'I spent a lot of my time looking at blue—no wonder I blue it!'

The music, especially in the first few bars, was inspired by Erik Satie's *Gymnopedies*, a trio of piano compositions that had no little influence on other rock musicians. Within the previous couple of years, the classical-rock fusion group Sky and electro-pop pioneer Gary Numan had both recorded and released material based on Satie's music, as had American jazz-rock outfit Blood, Sweat & Tears ten years earlier. In addition to the obvious Satieisms, a few sparing flourishes of lead guitar, and the rhythm section provide a relaxed beat almost verging on reggae, echoing the feel of 'Them Heavy People' on the previous album.

It was released as the second single from the album in Japan and Canada. The latter territory also issued a promotional copy with mono version on one side and stereo on the other on the Harvest label, pressed on (inevitably) blue vinyl.

2. 'In Search of Peter Pan' 3.46

The first of Kate's seven songs dating back to 1976 or before, the song reflects her thoughts about childhood, and in particular J. M. Barrie's children's classic *Peter Pan*, which is mentioned by name and which she called 'an absolutely amazing observation on paternal attitudes and the relationships between the parents—how it's reflected on the children ... how a young innocence mind can be just controlled, manipulated, and they don't necessarily want it to happen that way'.[4]

Introduced by a few seconds of delicate tinkling piano that sound like an old-fashioned music box, its lyrics refer to comforts provided by the elder generation—'Granny takes me on her knee, she tells me I'm too sensitive'— and of childhood dreams—'When I am a man I will be an astronaut'. The atmosphere of a young person's world of make-believe is enhanced by an ethereal vocal sounding like a children's choir, and near the end, the quoting of a couple of lines from the last verse of the song 'When You Wish Upon a Star' by Leigh Harline and Ned Washington, written for the Walt Disney film *Pinocchio* in 1940.

3. 'Wow' 3.58

Kate had intended to write a song about the music business, 'not just rock music but show business in general, including acting and theatre. People say that the music business is about ripoffs, the rat race, competition, strain, people trying to cut you down, and so on, and though that's all there, there's also the magic. It was sparked off when I sat down to try and write a Pink Floyd song, something spacey.'[5] To some extent, it was also a tale of the solo performer's basic insecurity in the spotlight, 'we're all alone on the stage tonight'.

Reflecting on the presence of several gays in show business, acting, and theatre, the lyrics include a line referring to a well-known sexual lubricant, 'He's too busy hitting the Vaseline'. (Such use of a trade name in a song lyric alone would have been enough a few years earlier for the BBC to ban from broadcasting, or at least insist on a re-recording, as in the case of The Kinks' 'Lola' and its mention of Coca-Cola, hastily changed to the fictitious cherry-cola). In the original video, featuring her performing the song in a darkened studio, and then backed by spotlights during the chorus, she cheekily patted her behind while singing the line. Although this was barely commented on at the time, it was replaced on a video compilation released seven years later with what was considered a less risqué montage of her performing live in concert. Also given a namecheck was a popular British TV police drama series of the time, in the line 'He'll never make the screen, he'll never make *The Sweeney*'.

When she wrote it, she had not envisaged performing it live, but it took her only half an hour to devise a routine while preparing for a TV show in New Zealand. At the last concert of the tour at Hammersmith, she was highly amused when she sang it and a frogman appeared through the dry ice, one of the crew's last-night pranks, remarking afterwards, 'I'd have liked to have had it in every show.'[6]

The album's second single, it reached No. 14 in Britain in March 1979. Like the album, it had benefited from added exposure afforded by the Tour of Life that began shortly after release. It was well received by the media, with *Melody Maker* calling it 'the most precisely focused Kate Bush single since "Wuthering Heights" despite the self-indulgent lush production', while the *Guardian* called it the 'undisputed highlight' of the whole record. Only *Sounds* demurred, with a reference to 'this mediocre chanteuse crooning her way through this silly song'.

Issued as a single throughout most other countries, some chose to edit it slightly, generally omitting the first twelve seconds of synthesiser chords. Canada and Brazil were among the markets that used the full-length album version, the Canadian one in orange vinyl. Some twenty years later, in 2002, it was featured in the Rockstar North video game *Grand Theft Auto: Vice City*.

4. 'Don't Push Your Foot on the Heartbrake' 3.12

The track that Kate said was written as a 'Patti Smith song' was perhaps the closest she ever came to hard rock, at least on the chorus. Forty-five seconds in, what has started off as a mid-tempo number on the first verse hits full throttle on the chorus with some incisive guitar and drums, peaking on the third chorus with a 'Come on, you got to use your flow!' delivered in an impassioned shriek, half Lene Lovich, half Robert Plant, before bowing out with a calm coda on the piano. The lyrics refer to a character called Emma, who is put out on the road, perhaps a metaphorical one, and about to veer dangerously out of control—'Don't put your blues where your shoes should be'.

In addition to the album version and the live recording made at Hammersmith Odeon on the tour, first released on the *On Stage* EP, a demo version from 1977 was released on various bootleg CDs.

5. 'Oh England My Lionheart' 3.10

The almost-title track of the album is an unashamed paean of nostalgia, described by Kate as 'a sort of poetical play on the, if you like, the romantic visuals of England'.[7] In just over three minutes, against a completely acoustic, appropriately restrained musical backdrop with a touch of renaissance music about it, she evoked a thoroughly charming sense of national identity—London Bridge in the rain, Shakespeare on the rolling Thames, ravens in the tower, and wassailing in the orchard. It was a song that risked being dismissed as full of reactionary platitudes and a lament for the old world, as she knew.

In conversation with Harry Doherty at the time of the album's release, she said she appreciated that people might say it was sloppy: 'It's very classically done. It's only got acoustic instruments on it and it's done almost madrigally.... Everything I do is very English and I think that's one reason I've broken through to a lot of countries. The English vibe is very appealing'.[8] Very rarely, if ever, did she evoke better the spirit of pastoral England, a place of largely tranquil visions but with an undercurrent of darkness at the same time: 'Dropped from my black Spitfire to my funeral barge'.

Some years later, she all but disowned the song as embarrassing. It might have been an easy target for those who wanted to deride it as a Colonel Blimp-like yearning for a return to Victorian ways and values, but over forty years later, to these ears at least, it has lost none of its charm. Nobody ever criticised Ray Davies and The Kinks for their similarly affectionate look at a departed world in their classic album *The Village Green Preservation Society* ten years earlier.

6. 'Full House' 3.14

The second of the three songs written in 1978, this could have been a partly autobiographical look at the psychological problems that came with fame, with paranoia and self-doubt. It is sung from the slightly surreal point of view of someone driving herself home on a dark wet night, suddenly seeing herself in the road in front of her trying to get out of the rain—'I am my enemy, mowing me over'. The scene is set for an interesting scenario and a potentially interesting track, rather like the opening moments of a thriller. She resolves to get a grip, controlling her highs and her lows, questioning all that she does, 'trying to get back to the rudiments', but somehow the idea fails to gel. Is she looking at the person she has just become and does not like very much, who has 'a full house in [her] head tonight', the new Kate whose rapid success has taken her unawares, looking at what the pressures of stardom have made her or are threatening to turn her into?

Melodically, it is based around a progression of mostly minor chords and a little short on tune. The backdrop of tinkling piano and sturdy, occasionally pungent electric guitar and drums drive it along with some force, but fail to give much of a lift to what is probably the album's least musically interesting three minutes.

7. 'In the Warm Room' 3.35

It amused Kate that she was often accused of being a feminist, as she insisted she wrote a lot of her songs for men. This was one she cited as an example, one that would make a change from the preponderance of ones written 'for women about wonderful men that come up and chat you up when you're in the disco'. She recognised that she was probably female-oriented with her songs 'because I'm a female and have very female emotions but I do try and aim a lot of the psychology, if you like, at men.'[9] Alongside 'Feel It', this was one of her most unashamedly erotic tunes, with lines about how 'in the warm room she'll touch you with your Mamma's hand', 'her perfume reaches you', and, most tellingly, as she prepared for bed, 'she'll let you watch her undress, go places where your fingers long to linger'. Again, on a musical level, it is simplicity itself, a gentle number that only requires her piano as accompaniment.

It was her first choice when she was asked to perform on *Ask Aspel*, a children's TV programme. Not surprisingly, the BBC felt it was hardly pre-watershed fare, so she chose to sing the next track on the album instead. It must have amused her to be able to get away with substituting a song on a theme that was equally off limits (particularly in the 1970s) for young audiences, but avoided disapproval as it was nowhere near so explicit.

8. 'Kashka from Baghdad' 3.55

Kate had the idea for this song by 'a very strange American detective series' on TV, a musical theme that was regularly featured, and an old house. This led to the concept of an old house inhabited by two people, about whom nobody knew anything. As they lived in a small town, all the neighbours were consumed with curiosity, 'and these particular people in this house had a very private thing happening' (this had to be discreet as it went out in an early evening live phone-in interview on Radio 1).[10] They were in fact a gay couple who kept strictly to themselves for obvious reasons. Old friends never called there, and some wondered if there was any life inside the house at all. An element of voyeurism is supplied by the cryptic reference to the narrator who 'watch[es] their shadows tall and slim in the window opposite.'

The backing is quite simple, with the only adornment to Kate's piano, plus bass and drums, is an unobtrusive eastern *strumento da porco*, a stringed instrument of the zither family, played by her brother, Paddy.

9. 'Coffee Homeground' 3.38

A black comedy of a murder mystery set to music that could almost have been straight out of Bertolt Brecht and Kurt Weill's *Threepenny Opera* comes next. Some have said that there is an element of the Dr Crippen mystery in the lyrics, especially as there is a reference to 'pictures of Crippen'. Others point to a short story by Roald Dahl, *The Landlady*, about an elderly eccentric woman with a stuffed dog and parrot, her deceased pets, who murders her paying guests (fortunately for them, very few and far between) by poisoning them.

Kate said that it was written that summer, inspired by an American cab driver 'who was in fact a bit nutty'. The person in the story thinks they are being poisoned by somebody with arsenic or belladonna in their wine, so no, they do not want any coffee home-ground to follow, thank you. It was a deliberate attempt at 'a humorous aspect of paranoia' performed in Brechtian style to emphasise the humour, with a synthesiser evoking inter-war German musical theatre and an exaggerated vocal in the style of Lotte Lenya, Weill's wife—including a couple of phrases in German for good measure. Interestingly, when the first demos were recorded, the song had a different treatment entirely. Only as it gradually took shape did Kate have the idea of recording it with a German flavour.

10. 'Hammer Horror' 4.39

A song about murder—or at least a paranoid would-be murder victim—is followed by a ghost story. Assertions that it was meant to be about Hammer Films are incorrect. Kate said it was 'inspired by seeing James Cagney playing the part of Lon Chaney playing the hunchback—he was an actor in an actor in an actor, rather like Chinese boxes, and that's what I was trying to create.' It was about an actor and his friend, playing the lead in a production of *The Hunchback of Notre Dame*, a part he had been reading all his life, longing for the chance to play it. At last came his chance to take the starring role, but after several rehearsals, he died in an accident, and the friend accepted an offer to step into the role. The dead man returned to haunt him as he did not want him to have the part, believing he has taken away the only chance he ever wanted in life. The actor begged him to leave him alone, as it was not his fault; he had to take the role, but after this, he feared it was not the right thing to do, because the ghost would not leave him alone and was really freaking him out. Every time he looked round a corner, he was there, and never disappeared.[11]

The portentous introduction, a bombastic flourish from the strings and a few striking piano chords rather reminiscent of early Electric Light Orchestra, set the tone for the song. At the end, there are a few surreal effects and the sound of a gong to finish off.

Released as the first single on 27 October 1978, a couple of weeks before the album, it fared poorly, struggling only to No. 44. In other countries, it fared better, reaching the Top 10 in Ireland and Top 20 in Australia. A video was made featuring Kate and a masked dancer performing the song against a black background.

When Kate and the KT Bush Band recorded the original demo at her home studio prior to the album sessions, she told them that she needed to be genuinely frightened in order to 'get into the role'. Paddy decided that they ought to black the studio out, then he threw some lighted matches past the windows, and the others made ghostly noises while she was singing. It worked too well. She duly screamed in terror, lost her voice, and could not sing any more—so she had to return to the song a couple of days later.

Never for Ever

UK: Released 7 September 1980, EMI, No. 1 (one week)
US: 1980, EMI America
Personnel: Kate Bush: vocals, piano, keyboards, harmony vocals, Fairlight CMI digital sampling synthesizer, Yamaha CS-80 polyphonic synthesizer (1, 4), arranger

John L. Walters, Richard James Burgess: Fairlight CMI programming

Max Middleton: Fender Rhodes (1, 3, 5, 6, 10), Minimoog (5), string arrangements (3, 6)

Duncan Mackay: Fairlight CMI (4, 9)

Michael Moran: Prophet synthesizer (5)

Larry Fast: Prophet synthesizer (10)

Alan Murphy: electric guitar (1, 2, 6, 7–10), electric guitar solo (7), acoustic guitar (4), bass acoustic guitar (9)

Brian Bath: electric guitar (1, 6, 7, 10), acoustic guitar (3, 4, 9), backing vocals (6, 9)

Kevin Burke: violin (7)

Adam Skeaping: viola (8), string arrangements (8)

Joseph Skeaping: lironi (8), string arrangements (8)

John Giblin: bass guitar (1), fretless bass guitar (11)

Del Palmer: fretless bass (3), bass guitar (5–7)

Stuart Elliott: drums (1, 10), bodhran (9)

Preston Heyman: percussion (2, 3, 5), drums (3, 5–7), backing vocals (4, 6)

Roland: percussion (2)

Morris Pert: timpani (4), percussion (10)

Ian Bairnson: bass vocals (2)

Gary Hurst: backing vocals (1, 4)

Andrew Bryant: backing vocals (4)

Roy Harper: backing vocals (11)
Martyn Ford Orchestra: strings (3, 6)
Paddy Bush: backing vocals (1, 4–6, 9), balalaika (1), sitar, bass vocals and voice of Delius (2), koto (4), strumento de porco (psaltery) (5), harmonica and saw (6), banshee (7), mandolin (9)
Recorded at Abbey Road Studios and AIR Studios, London, September 1979–July 1980
Produced by Kate Bush and Jon Kelly

Kate's first two albums were to some extent recordings by a group, embellished as necessary—usually with strings—here and there. The first phase of her career ended, imperceptibly perhaps, with her production of the *On Stage* EP featuring four performances from the Hammersmith Odeon concert of 13 May 1979 (fans would wait another fifteen years for a full hour's worth of material to appear on record). When she returned to the studio as co-producer with Jon Kelly, who had engineered her previous work, she had decided to be more adventurous. While still composing her songs at the piano, she was eager to make use of new technology—particularly the Fairlight CMI (Computer Musical Instrument) synthesizer, a digital synthesizer, sampler, and digital audio station introduced only the previous year—so she could experiment with and expand her sonic horizons. Recording began in September 1979 after the EP was completed, and after a pause, it resumed early in the new year, with everything finished in May. Two songs, 'Egypt' and 'Violin', had been part of the Tour of Life setlist. Both of these, and 'The Wedding List', were featured in *Kate*, her Christmas 1979 TV special.

For once, it was not named after any particular track, but because 'all things pass, neither good not evil lasts. So we must tell our hearts that it is "never for ever", and be happy that it's like that!'[1] All things must pass, as the title song of a classic George Harrison triple album had already noted.

As co-producer, it represented a big step forward for her. About four years later, she remarked that it was the first album she had made that she could really sit back, listen to, and really appreciate now she had more of the freedom and control that she had craved ever since the start of her career.

On release in September, it entered the British album charts at No. 1, establishing several chart records. It was the first album by a British female singer to top the charts, the first one written entirely by the performer, and the first new studio album to achieve that feat. The only previous female vocalists to do so, Connie Francis and Barbra Streisand, were both American and both had done so with greatest hits compilations (in the latter's case, with a soundtrack album as well), as had one all-female group, Diana Ross and the Supremes. Three tracks were released as singles, one reaching the Top 10 and the other two Top 20.

The striking cover design, by Nick Price, showed various animals and monsters emerging from under her skirt. It was, she said, an illustration of 'the good and bad things that emerge from you'.

Tracks

1. 'Babooshka' 3.20

The opening track was the most successful of three singles from the album. It reached No. 5 in Britain, despite *Top of the Pops* being off the BBC TV schedules for several weeks at the time owing to a technicians' strike, and was certified silver by the British Phonographic industry for sales of over 250,000. In the lyrics, Kate tells of a wife's intention to test the fidelity of her husband by assuming the alter ego of Babooshka and sending him notes supposedly from a younger woman, which was how she feared was the opposite of how he saw her. A trap is set when, in her bitterness, she arranges to meet him while he is attracted to the character who reminds him of how she used to be earlier in their marriage.

Only after she had completed the song did she learn that '*babushka*' was the Russian word for grandmother, as well as a term for a headdress. While she was writing it, it was a name that simply came into her mind, and she thought she had got it from a fairy story she had read as a child. Then a series of extraordinary coincidences followed in close succession. She turned on the television, only to see Donald Swann singing his own song of the same title, thus making her realise that there actually must be somebody somewhere with such a name. Next she was looking through *Radio Times* and came across an opera called *Babushka*, co-written by Swann and Arthur Scholey (teachers ordering music for your pupils, take care you receive the item you really want). To cap it all, she then discovered one of her friends had a cat called Babooshka: 'So these really extraordinary things that kept coming up when in fact it was just a name that came into my head at the time purely because it fitted'.[2] Yet more strange phenomena indeed.

As a song, it was very commercial, with a distinctive chorus as well as a suitably, semi-oriental sound created by the combination of Brian Bath and Alan Murphy's guitars and Max Middleton's Fender Rhodes. The other musicians included John Giblin on fretless bass, another instrument that would contribute significantly towards the sound of her music in the new decade. At the ending came a sample of glass being smashed, one of the earliest examples of a sample created using the Fairlight. To obtain the required sounds, Kate, Jon Kelly, and John Walters (her Fairlight programmer, not the jazz musician turned BBC radio producer) created havoc in the Abbey Road studio by destroying glasses and sampling the resultant sound effects, then choosing and saving the best as digital files in the Fairlight memory. The final sound on the record is a slow arpeggio of such sounds played back through the keyboard. Their audio creativity did not impress the canteen staff along the corridor, lamenting the wanton destruction of their crockery, and a few individual boxes of Belgian chocolates were required to restore good relations.[3]

In the video, Kate appeared in the role of embittered wife in a black bodysuit and a veil, changing into an extravagant, myth-like, and rather sparse Russian-style costume as her alter ego, beside a double bass (contrabass) symbolising the husband. Her performance of the song in a Dr Hook television special, recorded in March 1980 and shown a month later, featured her in another costume as a staid Victorian lady in mourning dress on her right, and a contemporary young woman in silvery jumpsuit with lightning-streaks painted down the left side of her face. Her figure was lit so that only the dark side of her costume was seen during the verses of the song, and the glittering side in the choruses.

2. 'Delius (Song of Summer)' 2.51

Kate had been fascinated by the composer Frederick Delius ever since watching Ken Russell's film *Song of Summer*, part of the BBC TV *Omnibus* series, when she was ten years old. In old age, Delius was confined to a wheelchair and a young admirer, Eric Fenby, mentioned in the lyrics, acted as his unpaid assistant, taking down his compositions from dictation and helping him revise earlier works. She evokes a light-hearted, effortless feel in the song with piano and electronic percussion, although the lyrics are little more than a simplified chant and do not go very deep.

A video featuring her and Paddy Bush was shown on a Dr Hook television special on 7 April 1980 and during *The Russell Harty Show* on 25 November that same year. It portrayed an elderly man in a wheelchair partly covered by a rug, sitting on a peaceful English riverbank covered with reeds and grass, while a young girl in a gossamer white gown with wings glided along on the water.

3. 'Blow Away' 3.33

'Blow Away (for Bill)' was written as a requiem for lighting director Bill Duffield, who had been killed in an accident at Poole Arts Centre after the first date on the Tour of Life the previous year.

The phrase 'Put out the light, then, put out the light' is from Shakespeare's *Othello*, in the scene shortly before Othello kills Desdemona. A short roll call references other deceased musicians, all but one dead within the last two years, namely Minnie Riperton (another female singer with unusually high pitch), Marc Bolan, Keith Moon, Sid Vicious, Buddy Holly, and Sandy Denny—while 'Bolan and "Moonie" are heading the show tonight'. To some extent, it is about coming to terms with the Grim Reaper. Each of us, said Kate, had such a deep fear of death: 'It's the ultimate unknown, at the same time it's our ultimate purpose. That's what we're here for.... We're really transient, everything to do with us is transient, except for these non-physical things that we don't even control'.[4] A warm coating of strings with minimal piano, guitar, and drums supply gentle backing.

It received its premiere on 18 November 1979 in a concert at the Royal Albert Hall to celebrate seventy-five years of the London Symphony Orchestra, its sole live performance. A heartfelt number, although tribute songs run the risk of sounding either trite or mawkish, Thomson calls it 'whimsical but unengaging'.[5]

4. 'All We Ever Look For' 3.47

This is Kate's song about family relationships in general: 'Our parents got beaten physically. We get beaten psychologically'. The final line, 'All we ever look for—but we never did score' refers to having to face futile situations: '... you have to accept it, you *have* to cope with it'.[6]

Musically, it makes interesting use of the Fairlight, playing back several sound samples. At one stage, a group of Hare Krishna followers sings the 'Maha Mantra', with Kate using a tiny part of a line from the mantra: '(Hare) Krishna, Hare Krishna, (Krishna Krishna, Hare Hare)', presumably to represent the chorus immediately following the sound clips, 'a God', followed by birdsong ('A Drug') and then finally applause ('A Hug').

5. 'Egypt' 4.10

In Kate's own words, this was 'an attempted audial animation of the romantic and realistic visions of a country'. Kate explained that it was a song about disillusion. She visualised a person who had never been there and assumed that it was full of romance and the pyramids—until they arrived there and discovered what it was really like. 'It's meant to be how blindly we see some things—"Oh, what a beautiful world", you know, when there's shit and sewers all around you'.[7] Musically it is an attractive oriental sound, its softly played synthesisers merging gently with Paddy Bush's psaltery. The dreamy romanticism of her lyrics of 'Egyptian delights' and being in love with the country convey nothing of any dark underbelly lurking, but they are balanced with more equivocal descriptions of how 'The Pyramids sound lonely tonight, the sands run red in lands of the Pharaohs', and being 'busy chasing up my demon'. Not necessarily one for the Egyptian Tourist Board, then.

6. 'The Wedding List' 4.15

Musically one of the album's most dramatic and theatrical-sounding songs, this was inspired by François Truffaut's 1968 film *The Bride Wore Black* (*La*

Mariée était en noir). It is the tale of a groom who is accidentally murdered on the day of his wedding by a group of five people who shoot at him from a window. The vengeful bride hunts them down and kills them in a row, including the last one who is in jail. For Kate, the story was not just a savage drama in itself, but also a psychological study.

Revenge was a terrible power, she opined, 'and the idea is to show that it's so strong that even at such a tragic time it's all she can think about. I find the whole aggression of human beings fascinating—how we are suddenly whipped up to such an extent that we can't see anything except that.'[8]

7. 'Violin' 3.15

While Kate took violin lessons as a child, she found piano and organ much more to her liking and did not persevere with the instrument. This was one of her simplest lyrics with a much-repeated chorus and a brief reference to Nero, the Roman emperor, who according to legend played his fiddle while watching his capital go up in flames.

It was introduced to fans during the Tour of Life, as the eighth song of the first act. Not only violin but energetic electric guitar and drums also feature prominently in one of her most hard-rocking pieces, to say nothing of a few impassioned vocal acrobatics reminiscent of Siouxsie Sioux or Lene Lovich.

8. 'The Infant Kiss' 2.50

This was inspired by a Gothic horror film from 1961, *The Innocents*, based on Henry James' novel of 1898, *The Turn of the Screw*. A governess is frightened by the adult feelings she has developed for her young male charge—'What is this? An infant kiss that sends my body tingling?'—and she is possessed by the spirit of a grown man who believes that the ghost of her predecessor's dead lover is trying to control the bodies of the children she is looking after. A gentle number enhanced by a sensitive strings arrangement with prominent user of viola and lironi, it was also recorded in French with the title 'Un Baiser d'Enfant', released two years later (see p. 83).

A video was made by an American fan, Chris Williams, using scenes from *The Innocents*. When Kate contacted him after she had seen it, she told him he had chosen the exact scenes that she was thinking of while writing the song.

9. 'Night Scented Stock' 0.51

A brief interlude consisting almost entirely of layered vocals, this segues into the next track.

10. 'Army Dreamers' 2.50

Although Kate was sometimes derided by cynical journalists as being apolitical and in some way seemingly cocooned from contemporary social and political issues, in sharp contrast to some of her peers in the music business, the last two tracks on 'Never For Ever' – and significantly two of the three singles – showed a readiness to embrace the problems that were occupying the minds of so many of her generation.

The first of these songs, and the third single from the album in September 1980, peaked at No. 16. A waltz, it was the first song she had ever written completely in the studio. The subject is the effects of war, the waste of life that all too often follows when young men of school leaving age see military glory as their only chance of making something of themselves, and specifically about a mother grieving for her soldier son recently killed on military manoeuvres, 'putting the case of a mother in these circumstances, how incredibly sad it is for her. How she feels she should have been able to prevent it'.[9] Although the song was plainly anti-war, with a similar basic message to that of Elvis Costello's 'Oliver's Army' a year earlier, she stressed that she was not 'slagging off the army', as it was good for certain people, 'it's just so sad that there are kids who have no O-levels and nothing to do but become soldiers, and it's not really what they want. That's what frightens me'.[10, 11]

She performed the song on a couple of European TV shows, in Germany, to lip-synch the song as 'Mrs Mop', and in the Netherlands, dressed in military uniform. A video features her initially in close-up, dressed in dark green camouflage, blinking in synchronisation with the song's sampled gun cocks. She holds a white-haired child, who gets off her lap, walks away, and comes back as a young man in army combat uniform. Next she makes her way through woodland with other soldiers, braving explosions and reaching out for the initial soldier until he disappears, and at the end she too is killed.

11. 'Breathing' 5.29

Kate's second political song addressed the matter of nuclear war. It had been largely inspired by a documentary she saw about its effects and aftermath, and to some extent by hearing Pink Floyd's *The Wall*. For her, it had reached the point when she heard their album that she wondered what the point was in writing songs anymore because they had already said everything there was to say. 'You know, when something really gets you, it hits your creative centre and stops you creating … there's something about Floyd that's pretty atomic anyway'.[12]

What she wrote as a result was her own 'warning and plea from a future spirit to try and save mankind and his planet from irretrievable destruction'. Some of her songs were written and sung from the point of view of a third person, rather than herself. This is one of the prime examples, as she casts herself in the role of a foetus in its mother's womb, terrified at the prospect of imminent nuclear fallout. It has its senses—sight, smell, touch, taste, and hearing, and therefore knows what is going on outside the mother's womb.

It desperately wants to carry on living, as does the rest of mankind. 'Nuclear fallout is something we're all aware of, and worried about happening in our lives, and it's something we should all take time to think about. We're all innocent, none of us deserve to be blown up'.[13] The message thus cuts two ways, dealing with the reliance of an unborn baby on its mother, and also the vulnerability of the human race against those who hold the key to nuclear warfare in their hands. Her lyrics also refer to the foetus as it helplessly absorbs nicotine from the mother's smoking.

At the time, she thought the song was her best work to date:

> … because I think every writer, whether they admit it or not, loves the idea of writing their own symphony. The song says something real for me, whereas many of the others haven't quite got to the level that I would like them to reach, though they're trying to. Often it's because the song won't allow it, and that song allowed everything that I wanted to be done to it.[14]

The creative process of building the recording up was also enormously exciting for her. The session players had their lines provided for them, and understood what the song was all about, but at first she believed they lacked the necessary emotion that the track was demanding from them.

> It wasn't until they actually played with feeling that the whole thing took off. When we went and listened, I wanted to cry, because of what they had put into it. It was so tender. It meant a lot to me that they had put in as much as they could, because it must get hard for session guys. They get paid by the hour, and so many people don't want to hear the emotion. They want clear, perfect tuning, a 'good sound'; but often the out-of-tuneness, the uncleanliness, doesn't matter as much as the emotional content that's in there.

For her, that mattered for more than what she called 'the technicalities'.[15]

Roy Harper, an admirer and close friend, sings backing vocals on the track. It also incorporates spoken words describing the flash from a nuclear bomb, describing the differences between large and small nuclear explosions, and the fireball that could be seen sucking up under it the debris, dust, and living things around the area, then becoming recognisable as the familiar 'mushroom cloud'.

A little more than halfway through, her vocal fades out, to give way to a recording of a man describing how a mushroom cloud is created. As he describes the flash as 'far more dazzling than any light on earth—brighter even than the sun itself', a group of male voices, including that of Roy Harper, sings, 'What are we going to do without? We are all going to die without'. A stately yet fierce guitar figure then comes in over the semi-ambient piano and rhythm section as the male chorus becomes louder, with Kate joining in, 'Oh, God, please leave us something to breathe!' It all ends with a sharp whoosh, as if a nuclear bomb is consuming and obliterating the area in which it has landed.

To date the longest track she had recorded, it was a striking example of how she was progressing beyond the straitjacket of a conventional singer-songwriter recording her albums with a small band and assorted session musicians, to utilising the studio as an instrument, taking advantage of new sounds and technology to produce ever more ambitious work.

The video featured her in a womb portraying a foetus. She performed it live, a solo piano version in a benefit concert in aid of The Prince's Trust in July 1982 and during a Comic Relief concert on 25 April 1986. In 1985, she donated the song to a various artists' compilation *Greenpeace: The Album*.

The Dreaming

UK: Released 13 September 1982, EMI, No. 3
US: Released EMI America 1982
Personnel: Kate Bush: vocals, piano (all except 4), programming, electronic
           drums, Fairlight CMI synthesizer (1, 2, 5–10), Yamaha CS-80 (2),
           strings (4)
           Paddy Bush: sticks (1), mandolins and strings (4), bullroarer (6)
           Geoff Downes: Fairlight CMI trumpet section (1)
           Jimmy Bain: bass guitar (1, 5, 10)
           Del Palmer: bass guitar (2, 4, 8), fretless and 8-string bass (7)
           Preston Hayman: drums (1, 3, 5, 10), sticks (1)
           Stuart Elliott: drums (2, 4, 6–9), sticks (4), percussion (8)
           Dave Lawson: Synclavier (2, 4)
           Brian Bath: electric guitar (3)
           Danny Thompson: string bass (3)
           Ian Bairnson: acoustic guitar (5)
           Alan Murphy: electric guitar (5, 10)
           Rolf Harris: didgeridoo (6)
           Liam O'Flynn: pennywhistle, uillean pipes (7)
           Seàn Keane: fiddle (7)
           Dónal Lunny: bouzouki (7)
           Richard Thornton: vocals (8)
           Eberhard Weber: double bass (9)
           Paul Hardiman: 'Eeyore' (10)
           Esmail Sheikh: drum talk (10)
Recorded at Advision Studios, Odyssey Studios, Abbey Road Studios,
Townhouse Studios, London, September 1980–May 1982
Produced by Kate Bush

Kate's fourth album was the first she produced herself and throughout which she had full control, and once it was completed she regarded it as her favourite by far. Although it entered the UK album chart at No. 3, the initial reception was largely critical, and after peaking in the first week sales fell off rapidly. Ironically, in America where her records were suddenly popular on college radio stations, it became her first to reach the Billboard Top 200. It was generally recognised as uncommercial, perhaps deliberately so; she herself admitted as much. With hindsight, it came to be regarded as a brave and daringly experimental work if not a very accessible one, remarkably ahead of its time with its elements of world music, shifting time signatures, unusual percussion, vocal loops, and samples. Despite the presence of three guitarists, most of what they added was not used in the end, and seven of the tracks feature no guitar at all. The result was to be an album created by 'adding layers and layers of light and shade rather than relying on full-blown band performances'.[1]

Lyrically, it was by and large a sombre piece of work. Three years after release, she said she always felt that in order to write something that has meaning, 'that you should be unhappy that you should be in some kind of torment'.[2] On occasion, she referred to it as her 'she's gone mad' record, while others called it 'the Kate Bush Leonard Cohen album'.

Recording took place over the best part of two years, using four different London studios and several engineers. 'Sat in Your Lap', the first to be recorded, appeared as a single in June 1981 and reached No. 11, while she was worked on the rest of the album at Abbey Road and Odyssey Studios. After long days in the studio, she took a break from the album in the latter part of 1981 and resumed work early the next year, on overdubs and other final touches throughout January to May, in Advision Studios. Towards the end of the sessions, she was working a minimum of fifteen-hour sessions in the studio, then going home to listen to rough takes of the day's work and plan what needed to be done the next day.[3] It included an eclectic roster of session musicians, including members of The Chieftains and Planxty, Rolf Harris, and Jimmy Bain, formerly of Rainbow and later of Dio.

All the material was relatively new, and it was the first of her albums for which no pre-1978 songs were considered for inclusion, let alone recorded. Lyrically, she called it a 'searching, questioning album', with its themes of frustration, self-doubt and even lack of confidence much of it preoccupied with about how cruel people could be to each other. With hindsight some years later, she remarked with surprise how angry her vocals sounded.

Three singles were released in Britain. After 'Sat in Your Lap' came the title track and 'There Goes a Tenner' the following year, both considerably less successful. 'Night of the Swallow' was a single release in Ireland, and 'Suspended in Gaffa' in various European countries. Nevertheless, it was recognised by this time that Kate was an artist, not a pop star. Brian Southall of EMI admitted that prior to its release, the company came close to invoking a contractual clause that gave them the right to refuse or return an album to the artist if they thought it failed to reach commercial expectations, but in her case, they could hardly reject it on the grounds that it contained no three-minute and thirty-second pop singles. Her response would probably be, 'I know. I didn't write one.'[4]

The front cover photo illustrates a scene from the lyrics to 'Houdini'. Kate is acting as the character's wife, holding a key in her mouth that she is about to pass on to him in a surreptitious kiss. Only the gold key and her eye make-up show any colour, the rest being in sepia. The man was bass player, engineer, and her then partner Del Palmer.

In terms of sales and hit singles, the album may have punched below its weight at the time. Nevertheless, general opinion is that it stands the test of time by still sounding fresh and innovative nearly forty years later, far more so than many other records made around the same era that have dated less well.

Tracks

1. 'Sat in Your Lap' 3.29

Kate and Del Palmer were among those who went to see Stevie Wonder in concert at Wembley Arena in September 1980. Instantly inspired by the sheer energy of his performance and meeting him backstage afterwards, next day she worked on some piano patterns she had recently arranged, set a rhythm on the Roland, and worked in the piano riff to the hi-hat and snare. The verse and tune fitted with a few lines of lyrics she had, 'I see the people working', 'I want to be a lawyer', and 'I want to be a scholar', and the rest were any words that happened to come into her head. She had some chords for the chorus with the idea of ad-libbing a vocal later. The rhythm box, piano, and backing vocals, 'Some say that knowledge is ...' followed, and after that the lead vocal in the verses, and spent a few minutes getting some lines worked out before recording the chorus voice.[5]

The lyrics dealt with feelings of existential frustration, with humanity's endless quest for knowledge, 'and about the kind of people who really want to have knowledge but can't be bothered to do the things that they should in order to get it.... And also the more you learn the more ignorant you realize you are and that you get over one wall to find an even bigger one'.[6] Another theory suggested that the song title hinted at the possibility of experiencing enlightenment through sex.[7] Throughout the song, Kate's voice travelled the highs and lows, from an oddly clipped staccato one moment to an almost hysterical scream the next. She said she could imagine the vocal being sung from high on a hill on a windy day, hence her references in the lyrics to the fool on the hill, or the king of the castle: 'I must admit, just when I think I'm king'. Musically, it was faster and more percussion-orientated than her previous work.

It featured Preston Heyman on drums recorded at The Townhouse Studio 2, London, and Paddy Bush and Preston on whip-like percussion, played on bamboo canes swooshing rhythmically through the air, as well as a Fairlight CMI trumpet section arrangement by Geoff Downes of Yes, Asia, and Buggles fame. At the time of writing and recording the track, they could hardly have foreseen that it would hit the record shops at a time when a similarly full-blooded drumbeat would be a major element in the sound of competing singles by Bow Wow Wow and 1981's biggest-selling group in Britain, Adam and the Ants.

The single version was remixed for the album, with the vocals raised higher and minor modifications made to the backing track to fit in better with the overall feel of the other tracks. The demo version included an additional first verse at the start, which was subsequently discarded.

In an era where 12-inch singles were becoming increasingly the norm, it was considered for issue in this format as well as the 7-inch, but cancelled. The B-side was a cover version, a first for her, of Donovan's *Lord of the Reedy River* (see pp. 82–3).

A video was made over two days, featuring Kate dancing with a group of characters dressed as spirits, some in jesters' costumes, and others all in white on roller skates.

2. 'There Goes a Tenner' 3.24

Apparently inspired by old films, the subject matter was a bungled bank robbery as related by one of the incompetent gang—cue memories of post-war Ealing comedies and the like. 'It's about amateur robbers who have only done small things,' she said, 'and this is quite a big robbery that they've been planning for months, and when it actually starts happening, they start freaking out. They're really scared, and they're so aware of the fact that something could go wrong that they're paranoid and want to go home'.[8] The reference to a 10-shilling note suggested that the action must have taken place around the middle of the twentieth century, and the accents in which she sang went from mock-aristocratic to mockney-speaking East End villain the next.

Seen as 'the great lost Kate Bush single', and evidently EMI's last half-hearted attempt to promote an under-performing album with a third single, on release it went unheralded by radio stations, a similar fate befalling the video on music television shows. With almost no media interest, it became her first single to miss the Top 75 in the UK, crawling in at No. 93 for one week. Once again, plans to issue it as a 12-inch single were cancelled as a result. A feeling that songs about using gelignite to blow up a bank safe were considered unsuitable for airplay may have made it *persona non grata* with radio producers. Four years earlier, the Sex Pistols' Top 10 hit 'No One Is Innocent', featuring guest vocalist Ronnie Biggs, who had taken part in 'the great train robbery' in 1963, escaped from prison and spent the next few years as a fugitive abroad, had been banned by BBC radio and TV on grounds of bad taste and a reluctance to glorify criminal activity.

The B-side, 'Ne T'Enfuis Pas' ('Don't Run Away') was misspelt on the label as 'Ne T'en Fui Pas'. It was issued as an A-side in France, with a sleeve insert featuring lyrics in French and English, the latter rendered as 'Don't Fly Away', and 'Un Baiser d'Enfant' on the B-side.

3. 'Pull Out the Pin' 5.26

Kate had seen a documentary about the Vietnamese war shot by an Australian cameraman on the front line. She was impressed by his portrayal of the people in Vietnam as a really crafted, beautiful race who treated their fighting as an art, and could literally smell the Americans coming through the jungle with their aroma of Coke cans, ice creams, sickly cologne, American tobacco, and stale sweat. Before they went into action, the Vietnamese popped a little silver Buddha in their mouths, so that if they died they would have Buddha on their lips. 'Grotesque beauty attracts me,' she said. 'Negative images are often so interesting.'[9]

The music was every bit as harsh as the subject matter. Kate's piano was supplemented by the rhythm section, including some adventurous string bass and eerily but effective discordant guitar, while her call and respond backing vocals and battlefield sound effects enhanced the bellicose atmosphere conjured up by the subject.

4. 'Suspended in Gaffa' 3.54

One of the more abstract songs on the album, this was broadly about the quest for personal fulfilment. A reference in the first verse to 'that girl in the mirror between you and me' suggested an image of self-doubt and alienation, followed by mentions of 'wanting it all'. The title was a subtle pun on gaffer tape, as used by technicians in film and production, and thus suggested being trapped in a metaphorical web. She admitted that, unlike most of her songs, it was 'reasonably autobiographical … about seeing something that you want— on any level—and not being able to get that thing unless you work hard and in the right way towards it'.[10] To some extent, it reflected her Roman Catholic upbringing, that gave her the imagery of purgatory and of the idea that once a person was taken there, they would be given a glimpse of God and then you would not see Him again until you were let into heaven.[11]

A quirky tune, for the most part it sounded like a fairground waltz, with touches of mandolin and strings supplementing a bouncy synclavier. The percussion was supplied by 'sticks' rather than full drums.

It was released as a single in Australia and most European countries, excluding Britain. In some countries, the B-side was 'Dreamtime' (which originally appeared as the B-side to 'The Dreaming'), released as a single in Europe and Australia, but not in Britain, where 'There Goes a Tenner' was released instead.

A video was produced, featuring her performing a dance in a barn—with a brief guest appearance from her mother.

5. 'Leave it Open' 3.20

Another introspective and fairly abstract song, the lyrics are full of a desire to acknowledge and express the darker sides of her personality. One simple statistic says much; the title appears five times in the song, the phrase 'Harm is in us' over twenty. She explained it as about being open and shut to stimuli at the right times: '… often we have closed minds and open mouths when perhaps we should have open minds and shut mouths'.[12]

A strident drum beat opens the track and continues throughout most of the song. On the demo she and the engineer used a Revox, and effects including a guitar chorus pedal and an analogue delay system. They intended to give the track an Eastern flavour and the finished demo had a distinctive mood. There are several different vocal parts, each portraying a separate character and therefore requiring an individual sound. When a lot of vocals were being used in contrast rather than 'as one', more emphasis had to go on distinguishing between the different voices, especially if the vocals were coming from one person.

Towards the end, the guitar and thunderous gated reverb on the drums explodes and then cuts out. Kate told Nick Launay that she wanted the latter to sound like cannons firing at them from across a valley, so he obtained some corrugated iron from a building site and put it around the kit. They experimented with making sound loops to achieve the right effect, he recalled, and it was 'like being in a toy shop'. The final part was a strange soundscape of distorted and reversed vocals, the final repeated line being 'we let the weirdness in'. A couple of years later, Kate revealed in a fan club newsletter that one American fan contacted her regularly for a while with different, increasingly bizarre guesses as to what he thought she was singing, his final one being 'we paint the penguins pink'.

6. 'The Dreaming' 4.14

The album's title track was released as a single in July 1982, her first for a year, but only reached No. 48 in Britain. It was also her third 45 within three years to address political and environmental issues.

Ever since she had visited the country during childhood, it had been her aim to create something a piece of music with a specific feel of Australia within it. Loving the sound of the traditional aboriginal instruments, as she grew up she became more aware of the situation that existed between the white Australians and the Aborigines, who were being wiped out by man's greed for uranium and digging up their sacred grounds—all for the sake of plutonium, and ultimately the arms trade.

Musically it was constructed on the pattern of a hard rhythmic tattoo. They started with the drums, working to a basic Linn drum machine pattern, making them sound as tribal and deep as possible. She wanted the song to try and convey the atmosphere of the wide open bush, the Aborigines, and the track 'had to roll around in mud and dirt, try to become a part of the earth'. The right imagery had to be evoked in sound—the Aborigines driven away as the digging machines moved in, destroying the sacred grounds, their beliefs in Dreamtime growing blurred through the contamination of modern civilization and alcohol. It was a situation that moved her deeply. 'Beautiful people from a most ancient race are found lying in the roads and gutters,' she said. 'Thank God the young Australians can see what's happening.'[13] Sparse chords are played on the piano to mark every few bars and each chord change. A few of Nick Launay's effects give the piano a wider, deeper tone, equivalent to voices in a choir. The wide open space was painted on the tape, and it was time to paint the sound that connected the humans to the earth, the didgeridoo, taking the place of the bass guitar and forming a constant drone, a hypnotic sound that seemed to travel in circles.

One fan online called it her 'proggiest moment', opining that it was the moment where she showed she was as good as Peter Gabriel at evoking an atmosphere in sound.

The record also gave Kate the opportunity to collaborate with Rolf Harris. She had always loved his 1962 hit 'Sun Arise', long since regarded as a seminal piece of world music. When he arrived at the studio, she explained the subject matter of the song, they listened to the basic track a couple of times to get the feel, and he picked up the didgeridoo, one from an armful he had brought to the studio with him. She said she had never heard a sound like it before, 'like a swarm of tiny velvet bees circling down the shaft ... and dancing around in my ear. It made me laugh, but there was something very strange about it, something of an age a long, long time ago'.[14] He played didgeridoo on the record, but she was disappointed at not being allowed to try and blow the instrument herself, as Aboriginal law forbade women to play it, and her hopes of striking a blow for womanhood around the world were dashed (she was perhaps unaware that there were female players of the instrument, but their playing took place 'in an informal context' and they were not specifically encouraged by Aboriginal elders). By way of consolation, he taught Paddy how to play it instead.

'Dreaming' was originally called 'The Abo Song' and 12-inch promotional copies were distributed, then recalled once it was realised that the title was arguably racist. The title, which does not appear in the lyrics, then came to her as she found a large volume on Australian lore, and was inspired by reading about Dreamtime, the time for Aboriginals when humans took the form of animals, when spirits were free to roam and in this song as the civilized begin to dominate, the 'original ones' dreamed of the dreamtime. The other word for it was The Dreaming—and there was the right name.

Kate's rhythmical breathing, coming in at thirty seconds in and again around the three-minute mark, and some of the drum sounds were sampled by Depeche Mode for their single 'Personal Jesus' in 1989. The former was open to misinterpretation, as one EMI employee at the time allegedly found her in the studio working on the hypnotic 'out-in-out-in' chant section of the track, and seemed outraged at the thought of her making an apparently X-rated record.

The deep sound on the chorus, Paddy Bush's bullroarer, is a device made from a ruler and a small piece of string, whirled round and round until it started spinning and winding the string up like a rubberband-powered aeroplane. The end result was a rhythmic growl, like a motorcycle, as it released the stored-up energy. A close listen, he said, would reveal the string snapping and hitting one of the Abbey Road soundproof screens. 'Wait till we do it on stage…'

The B-side of the British single, 'Dreamtime', is sometimes incorrectly referred to as an instrumental version. It omits all the sung lead vocal lyrics, but retains most of the backing vocals such as the stretched harmonies in the chorus, and has an extended intro and outro, starting with about four bars of double-tracked didgeridoo drone before the original arrangement comes in and finishes with thirty seconds of the same, followed by Harris saying 'we'll stop right there'.

7. 'Night of the Swallow' 5.22

From Australia to the Emerald Isle, this narrative song concerns a woman who is trying to prevent her man, a pilot, from accepting an illegal commission to fly some people into another country, with no questions asked. He finds the challenge probably more exciting than the job itself, is keen to fly away, and thinks he will be fine as he can hide the plane high up in the clouds on a night with no moon, and swoop over the water like a swallow. She threatens to tell the law if he does, but he insists that she must not stop him: 'Would you break even my wings, like a swallow?' She saw it as a story reflecting how many men felt trapped in their relationships as the woman was so scared, perhaps through insecurity, and needed to control him by hanging on to him completely.[15]

Kate being the daughter of an Irish mother, the music of the Emerald Isle had always exerted a strong emotional pull over her. Once she had written the song and the basic track was recorded at Abbey Road, she realised the choruses would be ideally suited to a ceilidh band. Having been introduced long ago to the work of Planxty by brother Paddy, she phoned their keyboard player Bill Whelan to discuss it, sent him a cassette, and a few days later he had an arrangement ready. She and Jay went to Dublin, where they recorded at Windmill Studios with Liam O'Flynn on pennywhistle and uillean pipes, Dónal Lunny on bouzouki, present and past members of Planxty respectively, and Seán Keane of The Chieftains on fiddle, playing an arrangement written jointly by Kate and Bill. It was evidently a magical time for them all. 'As the choruses began to grow,' she said, 'the evening drew on and the glasses of Guinness, slowly dropping in level, became like sand glasses to tell the passing of time.' Planxty, she opined, were 'fantastic musicians with open, receptive minds, which is unusual for people who work with traditional folk music.' They cheerfully missed their plane and worked through the night. Next day, as she and Jay stepped on to the plane, she looked up into the sky and saw three swallows diving and chasing the flies.[16]

The track was appropriately released as a final single from the album in 1983, only in Ireland, with 'Houdini' on the B-side, but with scarcely any promotion, no video, and consequently no chart success. Ironically, the genre was in vogue at that time, for the best-selling British single of 1982 had been the heavily Celtic-flavoured 'Come on Eileen' by Kevin Rowland and Dexys Midnight Runners, whose album *Too-Rye-Ay* had gone back to Irish folk for its musical inspiration. To have put out 'Night of the Swallow' as a single in Britain in its wake might not have been such a bad move after all.

8. 'All the Love' 4.29

Yet another very introspective lyric, this is a song about feeling alone. 'The first time that I died' is the opening line of a paean to the difficulty of expressing love and letting others in, to the reality of being surrounded by people and friends much of the time, but still ultimately being alone. Kate intended to write 'about feeling alone, and how having to hide emotions away or being too scared to show love can lead to being lonely as well', about times when a person is unable to cope, cannot feel he or she can talk to anybody. 'I go and find a bathroom, a toilet or an empty room just to sit and let it out and try to put it all together in my mind. Then I go back and face it all again.'

One of her ideas for the song came when she returned from working in the studio late one night. She was checking her daily messages on the answering machine, which had recently developed a fault, speeding voices up beyond recognition. Her hope was that they would ring back again one day at normal speed. Instead, on this particular night, she began to play back the tape and the machine had edited half a dozen messages together to leave nothing but 'Goodbye', 'See you!', 'Cheers', and the like. It seemed odd for her to sit and listen to her friends ringing up apparently just to say goodbye. As she had several cassettes of peoples' messages all ending with authentic farewells, by copying them on to quarter-inch tape and rearranging the order, it was possible to synchronize the 'callers' with the last verse of the song. For a long time afterwards, some of her friends had not heard the album or recognised themselves and were puzzled as to how they managed to appear in the album credits without having even set foot in the studio.[17] It thus ends with a litany of warm, familiar voices of friends and family saying 'goodbye' on the phone, taken from real phone messages, while she hides behind her answering machine, contemplating 'all the love we should have given'.

Some thirty years later, journalist Jennifer Makowsky opined that the song was nothing less than a reminder of the value of staying connected to those we love, even when we are at odds with them, as we never know when tragedy may strike. The song's narrator is ignoring her own advice, waiting for her friends to contact her as the lines 'So now when they ring, I get my machine to let them in' capture the disconnection between humans amid an era of modern technology. In 1982, it was the telephone that brought people together and the answering machine that was the barrier between them. A faulty answering machine with a series of touching 'goodbyes' from friends came towards the end of the song. Later texting would replace the phone, becoming the primary means of communication and alienation, but the song still remained no less relevant and poignant.[18]

Musically it is one of the most simply-executed pieces on the album, with just her piano, bass guitar, drums, and the vocals of choirboy Richard Thornton, singing, 'We needed you to love us, too'.

9. 'Houdini' 3.48

Kate was fascinated by the life and afterlife of Harry Houdini, the renowned illusionist and escapologist who died in 1926, and this song is about the efforts of his widow Bess to contact him during spiritual seances after he had passed on. As shown on the album cover design, during his life, she had often helped him with his escapes by allowing him to pass the key to his chains to her in a kiss. Renowned for debunking spiritualist frauds during his lifetime, he had given her a code—'Rosabel, believe'—to ensure she knew it really was him. After his death, she made several attempts to contact him, and on one occasion, he came through to her, as reported by the press in January 1929. Later she came to believe that the code had been betrayed and she had been tricked. Kate thought it an astonishing idea that the man who had spent his life escaping from chains and ropes had actually managed to contact her. The image motivated her to write the song.

Before recording her vocal for the track, which musically has a setting mainly of ethereal strings and double bass, she drank a pint of milk and ate two bars of chocolate. Between them, they created a certain amount of mucus, in order to produce spit and gravel in the throat. As she sang the track, she and the engineer sped it up slightly so that when it was played back the voice would be a little deeper, and have more weight in it.

Its only release on single was as the B-side of the Irish single 'Night of the Swallow'.

10. 'Get Out of My House' 5.25

The album ends on a disturbing note, taking as inspiration Stephen King's novel *The Shining*, which Kate admitted was at that time the only book she had read that had really frightened her. The song uses the house as a metaphor for a person, a building that has become possessed, and has been locked and bolted to prevent any outside forces from entering. The woman has been hurt and decides she must keep everybody out, even to the extent of planting a concierge at the front door to stop any determined callers from passing, but the 'thing' still enters the house upstairs. It descends in the lift, and then approaches the door of the room where she was hiding.

She is in the house, explains Kate, trying unsuccessfully to get away from the object, so she changes physical form, initially into a bird trying to take flight—until the thing itself changes into a wind. The only solution therefore is 'to turn around and face it'. Some interpreted the lyric as an expression of hidden anger, the voice of a woman who has been intruded upon and had her privacy and sanctuary violated. It works as an indirect comment on the invasive nature of fame, remaining one of the most effective examples of her darkest fears and latent instincts.[19]

To accompany this tale of madness, or something verging on it, the instrumentation is very sparing, with mostly guitar and powerful drums, while bass, piano, and synthesiser play a less powerful role. Kate plays the role of a hysterical woman locking up her house, a contemplative soul singing, 'I wash the panes, I clean the stains', and a concierge primly saying, 'Honey won't let ya in for love, nor money'. Next, a man appeals to the woman to be allowed in, 'Let me bring in the devil dreams'. Finally, along comes Eeyore, braying 'hee haw' (get it?), ending up in a barely decipherable chant. It makes a strange, oddly wonderful and fitting conclusion to her 'I've gone mad' album.

Hounds of Love

UK: Released 16 September 1985, EMI, No. 1 (three weeks)
US: Released 1985, EMI America, No 30
Personnel: Kate Bush: vocals, Fairlight synthesizer, piano
             Alan Murphy: guitar (1, 3, 8)
             Del Palmer: LinnDrum programming, bass guitar (1, 10, 12),
             handclaps (3), backing vocals (5), Fairlight bass (8)
             Paddy Bush: balalaika (1), backing vocals (5), didgeridoo (3),
             harmony vocals (7) violins, fujara (12)
             Stuart Elliott: drums (1, 2, 4, 5, 9–11)
             Charlie Morgan: drums (2, 3, 5, 8, 10), handclaps (3)
             Jonathan Williams: cello (2)
             Martin Glover: bass guitar (3)
             Morris Pert: percussion (3)
             Eberhard Weber: bass guitar (4, 11)
             The Medici Sextet: strings (5)
             Dave Lawson: string arrangements (5)
             Brian Bath: backing vocals (5), guitar (11)
             John Carder Bush: backing vocals (5), narration (10)
             Dónal Lunny: bouzouki (6, 10, 11), bodhran (10)
             John Sheahan: whistles (6, 10), fiddles (10)
             Kevin McAlea: synthesizer, sequencer (8, 12)
             Danny Thompson: double bass (9)
             Liam O'Flynn: uillean pipes (10, 11)
             The Richard Hickox Singers: choir (11)
             Richard Hickox: vocals, choir master (11)
             Michael Berkeley: vocal arrangements (11)
             John Williams: guitar (12)
Recorded at Wickham Farm Home Studio, Welling; Windmill Lane Studios,
Dublin; Abbey Road Studios, London, November 1983–June 1985

Produced by Kate Bush

The Dreaming had been an expensive and exhausting album to make, and its modest success had not gone unnoticed by a cost-conscious EMI. Physically and mentally drained by the experience, unable to write songs for several months, once it had been completed, Kate took a break to lead a more normal lifestyle for a few months, away from the pressures of work. The following year, she had the studio in the barn behind her family home upgraded to a professional forty-eight-track facility that she could use at will, free from the expense and constraints of having to record in London. Demos for the next album were made there, and instead of being discarded with songs re-recorded from scratch, these were kept, enhanced during sessions, overdubbed, and thus developed into the final versions.

The record would be divided into two parts. Side one consisted of five standalone songs, side two a suite of seven numbers, 'The Ninth Wave', based around the story of a girl alone in the water for the night as she contemplated her past, present, and future in order to stay awake, to stop herself them from going to sleep and drowning, until rescue arrived next morning.

Heavy exposure on radio and TV for the lead-off single, 'Running Up That Hill', which peaked at No. 3, was followed by a launch party for the album at London Planetarium on 5 September at which invited guests were treated to a playback as they watched a laser show inside. Eleven days later, the album was released, and became her second to enter the British chart at No. 1, staying there for three weeks. Single and album both made the American Top 40, one place where her records had previously never fared well. The critical reception was almost overwhelmingly positive, and to this day, it is generally regarded as her all-time masterpiece. Its success gave her the passport to pursue her own career path as a recording artist from then onwards, without pressure from EMI. 'They left me alone from that point,' she said bluntly three years later. 'It shut them up.'[1]

In June 1997, a remastered version appeared on CD as part of EMI's 'First Centenary' reissue series. It included six bonus tracks, namely 12-inch mixes of 'The Big Sky' and 'Running Up That Hill', and the B-sides 'Under the Ivy', 'Burning Bridge', 'My Lagan Love', and 'Be Kind to My Mistakes'. Seventeen years later, in her *Before the Dawn* concerts at the Hammersmith Odeon in 2014, she performed most of the album's tracks on stage live for the first time, except 'The Big Sky' and 'Mother Stands for Comfort'.

Tracks—Side One: 'Hounds of Love'

1. 'Running Up That Hill (A Deal With God)' 5.03
Kate's first new record for almost three years was released as a single on 5

August 1985. EMI had wanted 'Cloudbusting' to be the first 45, but in a similar instance to the events of seven years earlier, she argued the case for this instead. On the same day, she performed it on Terry Wogan's BBC1 TV chat show, a favourite of her mother. It entered the UK chart at No. 9, peaked at No. 3, remaining her most successful British 45 since 'Wuthering Heights', as well as her breakthrough American hit, reaching No. 30 in the Billboard chart (as subsequently did the album).

Written in one evening, two years earlier, it became the first item to be recorded at what would become sessions for the album. An ethereal Fairlight drone is joined by electronic drums beating out a tattoo-like pattern, all programmed by Del Palmer and acting as the basis for the initial recording. Further work took place in November and early December, with Alan Murphy on guitar, Stuart Elliott on drums, and Paddy Bush on balalaika. Gradually it became evident that here was a new, more mature Kate Bush. One reviewer, admittedly writing with hindsight nearly thirty years later, would observe that 'gone was the wide-eyed, shrill-voiced *ingénue* of "Wuthering Heights", now with a deeper, richer voice, her movements more controlled and self-possessed, [but] sensuous, anthemic and as spellbinding as ever,' with a new single that 'represented [her] at the peak of her powers'.[2]

Its creator described the song as being about the intense relationship between a couple who could not really see things from each other's point of view. Desperately concerned that something will go wrong between them, they decide that the solution is to make a deal with God to swap places— the man becoming the woman and *vice versa*—and they would thus come to understand their feelings much better. Her original, and preferred, choice of title had been 'A Deal with God', until EMI warned her that to mention God in the title would mean no airplay in several countries throughout the world. She bowed to pressure as far as the single was concerned, although allowed a double title for the song on the album (she could perhaps have cited The Beach Boys' 1966 classic 'God Only Knows', another EMI release, as a record that did the same, yet never met with any opposition in a more censorious age and still became a worldwide smash). Having just spent two or three years making an album on which she really needed to prove herself again, she had no intention of sacrificing radio exposure and potential sales to her own stubbornness. 'But it's always something I've regretted doing ... normally I always regret any compromises that I make.'[3]

A video featured her performing choreographed routines with dancer Michael Hervieu, both in Japanese costume. MTV rejected it on the grounds that they only broadcast music videos where the performer was lip-synching the song, and used a clip of her appearance on the Wogan show instead. She performed the song live for the first time with David Gilmour at *The Secret*

Policeman's Third Ball, a comedy show for charity, in 1987. It was also featured as the main theme tune for the 1986 children's drama serial *Running Scared*, and on the soundtrack of the film *The Chocolate War* in 1988.

The B-side of the 7-inch single contained a non-album track, 'Under the Ivy'. The 12-inch single, her first, contains both, plus an extended remix and an instrumental version of 'Running Up That Hill'. It was also the only 7-inch vinyl Kate Bush single ever released in Peru, under the title 'Cuesta Arriba' ('De La Colina').

In August 2012, she released a new '2012 Remix', using the backing track of the extended version on the 1985 12-inch single, with new lead vocals, the track transposed down a semitone to fit her lower vocal range. It was premiered as part of the soundtrack for the Olympics closing ceremony later that month, for a dance performance where a 'hill' or pyramid was gradually assembled by dancers from giant white blocks, representing each of the Olympic events. On her website, she commented afterwards how thrilled and touched she was by everyone's reaction to the remix, thought the whole closing ceremony of the Olympics was extraordinary, wanted to thank all those involved for choosing her to be a part of it, and considered it 'a huge honour'. It entered the British chart at No. 6, reappearing two years later in the Top 50 after her *Before the Dawn* concerts. Although originally available only as a digital download, promotional CD singles were produced for the media. In April 2013, a 10-inch picture disc was made available for Record Store Day, with the original recording of 'Walk Straight Down the Middle' on the B-side.

In a retrospective some thirty years later, Alexis Petridis observed that, despite a hit-laden career, Kate was categorically 'not a singles artist'; it was impossible to get a sense of the scope and depth of her albums via the singles taken from them. If anybody had to choose one song that 'encapsulates her uniqueness,' this would be it, 'a track that simultaneously functions as pop and something infinitely stranger.... It draws the listener inexorably into its idiosyncratic world: pop music made by someone alive to the possibilities of what pop music can be'.[4]

Over twenty cover versions have been recorded, by acts including Tori Amos, Kiki Dee & Carmelo Luggeri, Will Young, Tiffany, Chromatics, Little Boots, Norwegian singer Jørn Lande, Dutch symphonic metal band Within Temptation, and Australian electro trio Infusion. The best-known, by Placebo, has been used regularly on TV programmes and film soundtracks, including *From Paris with Love* and *The Heavy*.

2. 'Hounds of Love' 3.02

'It's in the trees! It's coming!' These words, sampled from a scene from the 1957 British film *Night of the Demon*, spoken by actor Maurice Denham but mouthed by Reginald Beckwith, opened the title track, which in February 1986 became the third of four singles from the album, rising to No. 18. It is about the idea of people being in love, wanting to run away from and not to let it catch them or trap them, in case the hounds want to tear them to pieces. Love is portrayed as the personification of something coming to get them, and there is no choice but to run away. 'I wonder if everyone is perhaps ruled by fear, and afraid of getting into relationships on some level or another,' she mused. 'Maybe the being involved isn't as horrific as your imagination can build it up to being—perhaps these baying hounds are really friendly.'[5]

Kate directed the video of the song, inspired by Alfred Hitchcock's film *The 39 Steps*, with an extra portraying Hitchcock seen briefly in the first twenty seconds, as per his cameo appearances in his own pictures.

The B-side of the single in Britain was the non-album track 'The Handsome Cabin Boy' (see p. xx). The 12-inch single featured a remix, 'Alternative Hounds of Love', plus on the B-side 'The Handsome Cabin Boy' and 'Jig of Life'.

A cover version by The Futureheads was released as a single in 2005 and out-performed the original, reaching No. 8 in the British chart.

3. 'The Big Sky' 4.41

A sense of nostalgia pervaded this song, a look back at the simple, long-vanished pleasures enjoyed during childhood that adults could rarely find the time for, especially spending afternoons just watching the sky overhead and seeing the clouds taking on different shapes. Is there any person of mature years who has not done so when younger? Yet there was still the hint of a serpent in this or Garden of Eden. 'Come on and build me an ark,' says Noah. Is this a reference to the Old Testament story, or a veiled allusion to future ecological disaster?

Kate was not normally given to improvising or altering her songs once she had presented them to the other musicians, but this was an exception. With Alan Murphy on guitar, Youth of Killing Joke on bass guitar, and Charlie Morgan on drums, 'we accomplished quite a rock-and-roll feel for the track', all of them changing their arrangements dramatically between what they heard on the demo and the finished product:

We had a lot of trouble getting on together and it was just one of those songs that kept changing—at one point every week—and … it's not often that I've written a song like that: when you come up with something that can literally take you to so many different tangents, so many different forms of the same song, that you just end up not knowing where you are with it … a very strange beast.[6]

Haydn Bendall, engineer at Abbey Road Studios, agreed, saying that it went through 'three different incarnations'. To him, Kate was the ultimate perfectionist, working on one track for ages. Regardless of the cost in terms of time or money, if not satisfied she would retain her faith in the song and record it in a completely different way with different musicians.[7]

The fourth and final single from the album, released in April 1986, it reached No. 37 in the chart. British buyers had the choice of a 7-inch and 12-inch single, and a limited edition picture disc 7-inch. The first and third formats featured a special single mix on the A-side and non-album track 'Not This Time' on the B-side, while the 12-inch single consisted of an extended remix, 'The Meteorological Mix', on the A-side, plus 'Not This Time' and 'The Morning Fog' on the B-side. In the US, the B-side consisted of the special single mix of 'The Big Sky' plus 'Not This Time'.

The music video, directed by Kate, was filmed on 19 March 1986 at Elstree Film Studios, aided in the crowd scenes by a studio audience of about a hundred fans who had been invited and notified in advance of the shooting arrangements by the *Homeground* fanzine (see plate 11).

4. 'Mother Stands for Comfort' 3.07

After the first three wild and airy songs on the album, on this one the mood becomes very sombre. Musically, it is the least complex track on the album, with only Stuart Elliott's flat drum pattern, just kick and snare, and upright bass melody from Eberhard Weber backing Kate's vocal and piano, plus a few additional sounds from the Fairlight.

Kate admitted that 'the personality that sings this track is very unfeeling in a way'. It was in fact sung by a man who is a murderer, while resting assured that his mother's love would protect her, as she was fully prepared to defend him against anything. He was using her, as much as she is protecting him.[8] As the last verse goes, 'Mother will hide the murderer/Mother will stay Mum.'

5. 'Cloudbusting' 5.10

Kate returned to her fascination with the close relationship between psychologist and philosopher Wilhelm Reich and his son, Peter, told from the latter's point of view, full of imagery of an innocent child and yet being written by an adult, giving it a 'strange kind of personal intimacy and magic'. She had already visited the subject in her earlier song 'Symphony in Blue' (see p. xx). Here, she described the son's memories of life on their family farm, Organon, where father and son spent some of their time 'cloudbusting', using a machine designed and built by Reich Senior. He claimed that it could change atmospheric weather patterns, and cause rain when none had been forecast—a blessing to farmers when their crops were threatened by drought.

The song itself was primarily about how much the father meant to the son, how much he was missed when he was gone, and above all evoking the days of happiness when they were making it rain together. Some of the lyrics alluded to his arrest and imprisonment by the government, his sense of pain at his loss, and anguish at being unable to hide him from 'the men in power'. Having first read the book when she was much younger, she did so a second time and wrote the song as a result. Once it was finished, she sent a letter to Peter Reich saying what she had done, and to her delight received a very enthusiastic reply back from him.

The strings were played by the Medici Sextet, arranged by Dave Lawson, former keyboard player with Greenslade who had played keyboards on her previous album, with backing vocals by both Kate's brothers, plus Brian Bath and Des Palmer, and drums by Stuart Elliott, and Charlie Morgan. Musically, recording went according to plan until the ending when, in her words, 'everything just started falling apart', the drummer stopped and the strings would just sort of start wiggling around and talking, 'And then I thought maybe *decoy* tactics were the way, and we covered the whole thing over with the sound of a steam engine slowing down so that you had the sense of the journey coming to an end. And it worked, it covered up all the falling apart and actually made it sound very *complete* in a way. And we had terrible trouble getting a sound effect of steam train so we actually made up the sound effect out of various sounds, and Del was the steam. And we got a whistle on the Fairlight for the "poo poop."'[9]

The song, or rather the phrase, 'Ooohh, I just know that something good is gonna happen', was sampled by Utah Saints on 'Something Good', a No. 4 single in Britain in 1992.

EMI had initially wanted this as the first single from the album, but it was to become the second, on 14 October 1985, and reached No. 20. It was released as a 7-inch single, featuring 'Burning Bridge' on the B-side, and a 12-inch single in the UK and Europe, consisting of the extended 'Organon Remix' plus 'Burning Bridge' and 'My Lagan Love' on the B-side. In the USA, the 7-inch single featured 'The Man with the Child in His Eyes' on the B-side. The 12-inch single incorrectly called the extended version 'The Meteorological Mix', and featured 'The Man with the Child in His Eyes' and 'Sat In Your Lap' on the B-side. A promotional CD single was also made, featuring both the album version and the extended remix of 'Cloudbusting', plus the two B-sides. In 2019, a 12-inch picture disc featured the 'Organon Remix' and 'Under the Ivy' on side one, with 'Rocket Man' and 'Warn and Soothing' on the other.

The video, directed by Julian Doyle, was conceived by Terry Gilliam and Kate as a short film, made at The Vale of White Horse, Oxfordshire. Donald Sutherland portrayed Wilhelm Reich and Kate his son, Peter, seen on the top of a hill trying to make the cloudbuster work. Reich left Peter on the machine and returned to his lab. In flashback, he remembered several times he and Peter enjoyed together as Reich worked on various scientific projects, until interrupted by government officials who arrested him and ransacked the lab. Peter sensed his father's danger and tried to reach him, but was forced to watch helplessly as his father is driven away. Peter finally ran back to the cloudbuster and activated it successfully, to the joy of his father as he saw rain starting to fall.

Tracks—Side Two: 'The Ninth Wave'

The seven songs originally on side two of the vinyl release were a concept that Kate had based on her fascination with water. From this she developed the idea—or, as she saw it, a film—of a person being in the sea, the mystery of how they got there in the first place being unexplained. The basic idea was that they had been washed over the side of a ship so they were alone in the water, wearing a life jacket with a small light attached, to aid visibility should anybody else travelling at night would know they were there. Nevertheless, they were terrified, alone at the mercy of their imagination, and aware that they had to stay awake to survive, as falling asleep would be fatal.[10] The entire suite was performed in concert at the *Before the Dawn* shows.

Some were inclined to see it as partly autobiographical in concept. Reviewer Barry Walters suggested it was not, 'although its sink-or-swim scenario [could] be read as an extended metaphor' for the lengthy period it had taken Kate to write and record the whole album: '[Would] she rise to deliver the masterstroke that guaranteed artistic autonomy for the rest of her long career and enabled her to live a happy home life with zero participation in the outside world for years on end, or [would] she drown under the weight of her colossal ambition?'[11] Graeme Thomson saw it as 'a story about not dying, not going under, but instead riding the waves and, somehow, keeping going', with every moment of darkness and doubt balanced by a ringing affirmation.[12]

6. *'And Dream of Sheep'* 2.45
The first of these songs is about the person alone overnight in the water as darkness falls, awaiting rescue and fighting the impulse to go to sleep—'let me be weak, let me sleep and dream of sheep,' she sang. While writing it, Kate drew on childhood memories of having bad dreams when she was small, going into her parents' bedroom and her mother's side of the bed, not wanting to wake her, so standing there and waiting for her to sense her presence and the inevitable invitation 'Come here with me now.' Her mother voiced this line in the song, Kate having fully briefed her beforehand. An engineer they worked with picked out the line and said this was his favourite part of the album, as he found it so moving and comforting.

The song is a tender moment of calm before the storm. A careful listen will reveal the shipping forecast—'Bell Rock, Tiree, Cromarty'—sampled from the BBC, and the faint cries of a seagull.

Sessions for this and 'Jig of Life' were recorded partly at Windmill Lane Studios, Dublin, in the spring of 1984, with Donal Lunny on bouzouki and John Sheahan on whistles. In a remarkable display of perfectionism, she asked for the single whistle note at the end of the track to be played repeatedly for about three hours, as she wanted just the right 'bend' in the note.

She recorded a video of the song to be shown during the 2014 concerts while she sang live. The shoot involved working over three days in a special tank at Pinewood Studios, wearing a lifejacket and looking up at the camera waiting to be rescued.

7. 'Under Ice' 2.21

Memories of the past and visions of the immediate future have clouded the central figure's consciousness to the point where she can no longer distinguish between reality and illusion. The waterbound survivor inevitably goes to sleep despite all efforts to stay awake, and has a nightmare of being alone on a frozen lake and then trapped under the ice.

Kate found this a relatively simple song to compose and record. The tune she had composed on the Fairlight with the cello sound sounded very operatic, conjuring up an image of ice. With Paddy Bush on harmony vocals, it was completed in a day.

8. 'Waking the Witch' 4.18

In a song that had a flavour of medieval witch trials, Kate wrote of visitors who had come to wake the person or persons up, and bringing them out of their dream so that they did not drown. She was fascinated by the whole concept of witch-hunting and the fear of women's power, finding it 'very sexist behaviour ... female intuition and instincts are very strong, and are still put down, really. And in this song, this woman is being persecuted by the witch-hunter and the whole jury, although she's committed no crime, and they're trying to push her under the water to see if she'll sink or float.'[13]

The voices of her parents, brothers, Brian Tench (who mixed the album), Del Palmer, and Robbie Coltrane all contributed: 'It was just trying to get lots of different characters and all the ways that people wake you up, like falling asleep at your desk at school and the teacher says "Wake up child, pay attention."' Kevin McAlea supplied the synthesizer sequences while Alan Murphy was featured on guitar, Del on Fairlight bass, and Charlie Morgan on drums.

As the sound of a helicopter was required, she sought and obtained permission to use one from 'The Happiest Days of Our Lives' from Pink Floyd's *The Wall*.

Kate Bush, 1978. (*Croydon Picture Archive*)

Kate Bush, 1979. (*Croydon Picture Archive*)

Above left: 'Wuthering Heights', UK picture sleeve, 1978.

Above right: 'Wuthering Heights', Netherlands picture sleeve, 1978.

Above left: 'Wuthering Heights', Spain picture sleeve, 1978.

Above right: 'Wuthering Heights', Canada, 1978, where Kate's records were released on the Harvest label to 1981.

Above left: 'Moving/Wuthering Heights', Japan picture sleeve, 1978.

Above right: 'The Man with the Child in His Eyes', Netherlands picture sleeve, 1978.

Right: 'The Man with the Child in His Eyes', UK press advertisement, 1978.

'Hammer Horror', Japan picture sleeve, 1978.

'Wow', Netherlands picture sleeve, 1979.

STEREO EMR-20567

ケイト、もうきみの魔力になす術もない……

彩かな色を音楽でえがきあげた話題のナンバー「ブルーのシンフォニー」は美しく妖しい誘惑の序曲

ブルーのシンフォニー

SYMPHONY IN BLUE

ケイト・ブッシュ

Kate Bush

フルハウス

FULLHOUSE

[プロデュース＆アレンジ] アンドリュー・パウエル

¥600

Above: 'Symphony in Blue', Japan picture sleeve, 1979.

Below: 'Symphony in Blue/Hammer Horror', Canada, blue vinyl, 1979.

'Them Heavy People', Japan picture sleeve, 1978.

'Breathing', Japan picture sleeve, 1980.

Above left and right: 'Babooshka', UK picture sleeve, 1980.

Above left: 'Army Dreamers', UK picture sleeve, 1980.

Above right: 'December Will Be Magic Again', UK picture sleeve, 1980.

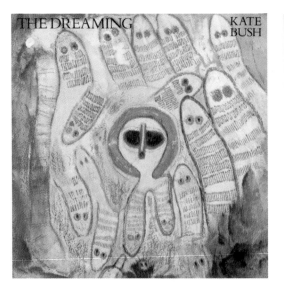

Above left: The Dreaming', UK picture sleeve, 1982.

Above right: 'Suspended in Gaffa', Netherlands picture sleeve, 1982, a single released in most European countries apart from UK and Ireland.

Night of the Swallow', Ireland picture sleeve, 1983. Release as a single was exclusive to Ireland.

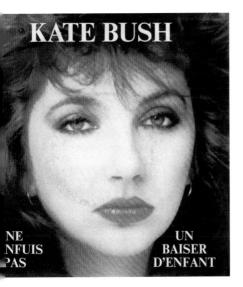

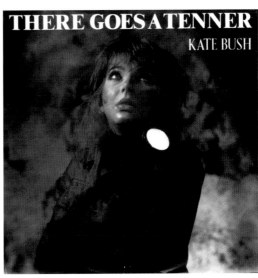

Above left: 'Ne T'enfuis Pas', France picture sleeve, 1983.

Above right: 'There Goes a Tenner', UK picture sleeve, 1983, her lowest charting single at home.

'Running Up That Hill', UK picture sleeve, 1985, her most successful single after 'Wuthering Heights'.

Above left: 'Cloudbusting', UK picture sleeve, 1986.

Above right: 'The Big Sky', UK picture sleeve, 1986.

Above left: 'Experiment IV', Japan picture sleeve, 1986.

Above right: 'Experiment IV', US 12-inch promotional single.

The video for 'The Big Sky' was shot on 19 March 1986 at Elstree Film Studios, Hertfordshire. Members of the Kate Bush Homeground fanzine were cast as some of the aviators, and the audience of about 100 fans who had travelled by coach from Manchester Square, London, was admitted for the crowd scenes. (© Paul Thomas)

Above left: 'The Sensual World', Japan promotional single, 1989.

Above right: 'The Sensual World', UK picture sleeve, 1989.

'Love and Anger', detail from UK picture sleeve, 1989, and first page of four-page section from a limited edition gatefold sleeve showing stills from the video.

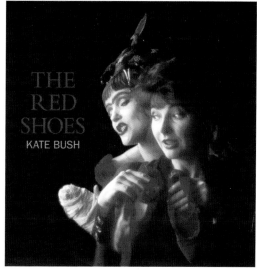

Above left: 'This Woman's Work', UK 7-inch picture disc, 1990.

Above right: 'The Red Shoes', UK picture sleeve, 1994.

'The Red Shoes', box comprising part of a UK promotional package sent out with the single and album to media and record shops, 1993.

Above left: 'Rubberband Girl', UK 12-inch picture disc, 1993.

Above right: 'Moments of Pleasure', UK picture sleeve, 1993.

Rubberband Girl', UK press
advertisement, 1993.

Four famous musical names in their own right who appeared on albums by Kate Bush from 1993 onwards.

Above: Eric Clapton (*Croydon Picture Archive*) and Gary Brooker (*Courtesy of Stefan Brendin/Creative Commons*).

Below: Prince and Andy Fairweather-Low (*both Croydon Picture Archive*)

Above left: 'King of the Mountain', UK 7-inch picture disc, 2005, featuring a drawing by Kate's son Bertie.

Above right: 'Lake Tahoe', UK 10-inch picture disc, 2012.

Kate Bush live at Hammersmith Odeon, 1 October 2014, at 'Before the Dawn' concerts. (© *Paul Carless*)

9. 'Watching You Without Me' 4.06

The unfortunate soul has been in the water for several hours, having been witch-hunted and suffered other indignities. At last they are kind of at home, in spirit, seeing their loved one sitting there waiting for them to come home, watching the clock, and obviously very worried about where they are, maybe making phone calls to try and find out. Even so, they cannot communicate, 'because they can't see you, they can't hear you'.

Kate found this really horrific, like her own personal worst nightmares put into song. When she and the musicians (mainly Stuart Elliott on drums and Danny Thompson on double bass) started putting the track together, she had the idea for the 'you can't hear me' backing vocals, and decided to disguise them so that the listener could not actually hear what she was singing.[14]

10. 'Jig of Life' 4.04

Kate wrote this in Ireland, based on a traditional tune that Paddy found and played to her, recommending that it would be ideal to incorporate at this point, being an uplifting piece of music that would pull the persons in the water out of despair. This is the stage of the story at which 'the future self of this person' comes to visit them and offer some help along the lines of 'look, don't give up, you've got to stay alive, 'cause if you don't stay alive, that means I don't'. She also found inspiration for using Celtic music in spending much of her time walking in the countryside at this time.[15]

As well as Stuart Elliott and Charlie Morgan on drums, and Del Palmer on bass, it also features John Sheahan on fiddles and whistles, Donal Lunny on bouzouki and bodhran, Liam O'Flynn on uillean pipes, and Paddy Bush on didgeridoo, while eldest brother, John, narrated the concluding poem. In 2014, when she performed this live during the *Before the Dawn* shows, a video of John appeared on a television screen, reprising the poem.

11. 'Hello Earth' 6.13

Kate found this a very difficult track to write, because it was in some ways 'too big for [her]'. At one stage, the result was a song with 'two huge great holes in the choruses, where the drums stopped, and everything stopped,' everyone else in the studio would ask what was going to happen in these choruses, and she had no idea until she hit on adding a vocal piece similar to the traditional tune she had heard used in the 1979 film *Nosferatu: The Vampyre*. Nothing she came up with could compare with what the piece was saying, and they did some research to find out if they could use it. They ended up re-recording the piece, and she made up words that sounded like what she could hear was happening on the original. Suddenly she could hear 'beautiful voices in these chorus that had just been like two black holes'.

The subsequent choral section, performed by the Richard Hickox Singers, was taken from the Georgian folk song, 'Zinzkaro' ('By the Spring'), which she heard performed by the Vocal Ensemble Gordela on the film soundtrack. In translation, the lyric reads, 'I was passing by the spring. There I met a beautiful woman with a jug on her shoulder. I spoke a word to her and she left, offended. I was passing by the spring.'

In some ways, she saw it as a lullaby for the Earth. To her, it was the idea of turning everything upside down and looking at it from above, like an image of someone lying in water at night and looking up at the sky all the time:

> I wonder if you wouldn't get the sense of as the stars were reflected in the water ... a sense of like, you could be looking up at water that's reflecting the stars from the sky that you're in. And the idea of them looking down at the earth and seeing these storms forming over America and moving around the globe, and they have this like huge fantastically overseeing view of everything, everything is in total perspective. And way, way down there somewhere there's this little dot in the ocean that is them.[16]

The musicians are Brian Bath on guitar, Eberhard Weber on bass, Liam O'Flynn on uillean pipes, Donal Lunny on bouzouki, and Stuart Elliott on drums. Opening the track is a ten-second excerpt from footage of a Columbia space shuttle mission, and it finishes with her whisper, 'Go to sleep, little Earth'.

It was used in an episode of the American TV series *Miami Vice*.

12. 'The Morning Fog' 2.34

A happy ending comes in the last song, or in Kate's words, 'now suddenly out of all this darkness and weight comes light'. Gone is the weightiness, the morning has come, and after the darkness of the previous track comes a brighter, more uplifting tone. Although nothing specifically says so, this is where they are rescued from the water. It was planned as 'one of those kind of "thank you and" songs', like the little finale 'where everyone does a little dance and then the bow and then they leave the stage'.[17] The musicians include Del Palmer on bass, Paddy Bush on violins and fujare (a Slovakian shepherd's flute), Kevin McAlea on synthesizer, and ex-Sky member John Williams on classical guitar.

6

The Whole Story

UK: Released 10 November 1986, EMI, No. 1 (two weeks)
US: Released 1986, EMI America, No. 76
Recorded 1977–86
Produced by Andrew Powell, Jon Kelly and Kate Bush

Coming hot on the heels of what had proved her most successful studio album to date, Kate's first and to date only greatest hits or 'best of' compilation was a perfectly-timed marketing exercise. She had been against the idea at first, concerned that it would be a poorly-packaged, mediocre sound quality affair, but realised there was some advantage in allowing the ever-supportive EMI some payback by not losing momentum while her commercial profile was at its highest. There would never be a better time, and she sensed that if she did it now she would never need go through it again.[1] As long as it was tastefully-packaged and properly planned, she would give it her blessing.

Heavy promotion on TV, radio, and in the press ensured that it would fly out of the shops, as it did. It stayed in the UK album chart for 126 weeks, two of them at the summit. Within a few years, over 6 million copies were sold on all three standard formats (LP, CD, and cassette), to casual buyers as well as dedicated fans—making it easily her most successful album. As with so many releases of a similar nature by other artists, at the company's request, it included a previously unreleased, specially recorded track to entice the completist, while the song that began it all was given a makeover. A home video compilation was released simultaneously, including the promotional videos for each song. The exception was 'Wow', where the original video was replaced by a montage of live clips, perhaps on the grounds that the old one of her patting her behind meaningly at the reference to the hero 'hitting the Vaseline' was a joke that had run its course.

Ten of the twelve tracks, namely (in order of appearance on the record) 'Cloudbusting', 'The Man with the Child in His Eyes', 'Breathing', 'Wow',

'Hounds of Love', 'Running Up That Hill', 'Army Dreamers', 'Sat in Your Lap', 'The Dreaming', and 'Babooshka' all faithfully reproduced the versions already available on album. They did not appear chronologically, as it was considered more important to equalise the running time on each side in order to obtain the highest quality pressing. It mattered less in America, where she was not so well-known and not everyone realised it was a compilation.

Far from regarding it as a cynical cash-in, the press was unanimously supportive. *Sounds* could pay it no higher tribute than commenting that it showed how Kate had 'matured into quite the most sensual, expressive, and creative artist this country can now boast'.

Side 1 (Track 1): 'Wuthering Heights (new vocal)' 4.57

While resisting the temptation to give all her early material a makeover, Kate had long thought that the original recording suffered from a production that was now dated, and her voice was too young. If time had allowed, she said, she 'probably would have done the same with a couple of [additional] songs'.[2]

The new version, about thirty seconds longer, boasts a more solid thump on the drums that makes the original sound almost tinny in comparison, and her vocal comes across as undeniably more mature. Another noticeable difference when comparing the old and the new is that on the former, her singing stops altogether at around 3.10 with the splendid marriage of Ian Bairnson's guitar and strings on the coda. Although the instrumental track is the same on the newer one, apart from allowing it to run on about thirty seconds longer, her voice makes a couple of brief returns at around 3.35 and again at 3.55, the latter more of a haunting, dramatic cry.

Comments online suggest that devotees are divided as to which is the superior version. The present writer, who usually thinks most remakes of classic oldies by the original artist rarely hold a candle to the originals, thinks that the newer, longer one sounds noticeably better without sacrificing any of the drama or uniqueness of the original, and benefits not only from a better drum sound, but also from the guitar solo being given more room to develop.

Side 2 (Track 10). 'Experiment IV' 4.21

The sole new track was one of Kate's most chilling yet. 'We were working secretly for the military,' runs the opening line, followed later by the confession, 'It's a mistake in the making.' Its theme was the tale of a group of scientists employed to work on a secret military plan, creating a sound horrific enough to kill people from a distance. The story was the not uncommon one of dedicated scientists so involved in their tasks in the pursuit of progress that they failed to appreciate how it might be used by unscrupulous powers, the classic example being of those who began splitting the atom, unaware of its possible future application as a weapon of mass destruction.

Playing alongside Alan Murphy on guitar and Stuart Elliott on drums is Nigel Kennedy on violin, deliberately mimicking the eerie sound of the instrument as in Bernard Herrmann's score for the shower scene in Alfred Hitchcock's 1960 horror classic film *Psycho*.

Although the conclusion was deliberately left vague, in the video almost everybody working on the project eventually succumbs to the sound. The aural Frankenstein to which they gave birth has done its terrible work to grim perfection. Featuring Kate and Del Palmer alongside a star-studded cast including Dawn French, Hugh Laurie, Richard Vernon, and Peter Vaughan, it chronicles the destruction of a secret military installation by a creature made of sound. Kate herself played an orderly officer serving tea, as the sound creature, and at the end entering a van. It was banned from *Top of the Pops* as 'too violent' for a pre-watershed slot, but shown at some cinemas as an accompaniment to the main feature.

It was released as a single in October 1986, reaching No. 23 the same week as 'Don't Give Up', a duet credited jointly to Peter Gabriel and Kate, from Peter's then-current album, hit a high of No. 9. The B-side was the new version of 'Wuthering Heights', while an extended remix (6.38), plus 'Heights' and 'December Will Be Magic Again', appeared on the 12-inch.

7

The Sensual World

UK: Released 16 October 1989, EMI, No. 2
US: Released 1989, Columbia, No. 43
Personnel: Kate Bush: vocals, piano, keyboards
             Del Palmer: Fairlight CMI percussion, bass guitar (1, 4, 7), rhythm
             guitar and percussion (5)
             Charlie Morgan: drums (1, 4, 6, 11)
             Stuart Elliott: drums (2, 3, 5, 7–9)
             Bill Whelan: arranger (on the Irish sessions)
             Paddy Bush: whip (swished fishing rod) (1), valiha (Madagascar
             tube zither) and backing vocals (2), mandolin (4), tupan (6)
             Davy Spillane: Uilleann pipes (1, 8), whistle (3)
             John Sheahan: fiddle (1)
             Dónal Lunny: bouzouki (1)
             John Giblin: bass guitar (2, 6, 9)
             David Gilmour: guitar (2, 9)
             Alan Murphy: guitar, guitar synth (3, 5, 7)
             Jonathan Williams: cello (3, 5, 7)
             Nigel Kennedy: violin (3), viola (5)
             Michael Kamen: orchestral arrangements (3, 5, 10)
             Alan Stivell: Celtic harp (3, 7), backing vocals (7)
             'Dr Bush' (Robert Bush, Kate's father): dialogue (3)
             Balanescu Quartet: strings, arranged by Michael Nyman (4)
             Mick Karn: bass guitar (5)
             Trio Bulgarka: vocals (6, 8, 9), arranged by Dimitar Penev
             Yanka Rupkina of Trio Bulgarka: solo vocalist (6, 9)
             Eberhard Weber: double bass guitar (8, 11)
Recorded at Wickham Farm Home Studio, Welling; Windmill Lane Studios,
Dublin; Abbey Road, London, 1987–9
Produced by Kate Bush

Kate followed the pattern established on *Hounds of Love* by recording mostly in her recently upgraded home studio with Del Palmer as her principal engineer, assisted from time to time by Haydn Bendall. She and Del had recently upgraded the studio, but for a while she felt overwhelmed by the equipment surrounding her, and made a conscious effort to try and move away from it, in order to 'treat the song as the song'. Having written some new numbers and realised she was not satisfied with them, but was going through a patch where she simply did not know what she wanted to say, she took a break for several months, then decided to begin work again on what she called 'ten short stories'. *Hounds of Love* had been two sides, one conceptual, but this was to be very much like short stories for her—saying something different in each one, or trying to paint each one as a different picture accordingly, as each had a different personality.

Writing and recording each one in the studio became part of the same creative process. In addition to the musicians with whom she and Del had worked for several years, various friends and renowned musicians were invited to come and augment the songs, among them Celtic harpist Alan Stivell, violinist Nigel Kennedy, and Mick Karn, of post-punk band Japan, known for his distinctive fretless bass playing. They would add their contributions to an existing backing track, and from these a composite of different takes would be used.

By the summer of 1988, most of the ten tracks had been mixed and an increasingly anxious EMI suggested that the album would be released that autumn, rather to her annoyance. She and an engineer decided that the songs and performances were not yet finished. Additional work took place, including some re-recorded vocals, guitar from Dave Gilmour, bass from John Giblin, and, most strikingly of all, additional backing vocals by the Trio Bulgarka, whose work had long fascinated her. In October 1988, she flew to Sofia to visit them and a week later they came to London, resulting in their appearance on three tracks, 'Deeper Understanding', 'Never Be Mine', and 'Rocket's Tail'. Editing and mixing continued until May 1989, plus final touches of overdubbing strings with Michael Kamen at Abbey Road.

Shortly after release, she commented that others had told her they thought it a very dark record, although she thought it was her happiest album to date. She admitted she had a dark sense of humour: '… maybe it is a subconscious thing that just goes into my music, because I think when I was writing this album that was perhaps something I was feeling a little—a sense of being a bit scared. Maybe it comes out in the music'. She also thought there was an element of self-therapy, in that the more she worked on an album, the more she felt it was almost a process for her to try and heal or have a look at herself: '… what artistic people are trying to do is work through their problems through their art—look at themselves, confront all these things'.[1]

Four of the songs were reworked some twenty years later for her album *Director's Cut*. A video collection, *The Sensual World: The Videos*, was also released, containing videos for the title song, 'Love and Anger', and 'This Woman's Work', all directed by Bush herself, with excerpts from an interview she gave on the music TV channel VH1.

In 1991, the album received a nomination for a Grammy Award for Best Alternative Music Album. She was nominated for two BRIT Awards in 1990 as Best British Producer and Best British Album of the Year for the album.

Tracks

1. 'The Sensual World' 3.57

Kate was inspired to write the song after hearing actress Siobhan McKenna reading the closing soliloquy from James Joyce's *Ulysses*, published in 1922, where the character Molly Bloom recalls her earliest sexual experience with her future husband, Leopold, as it seemed to fit the music well. Believing the text to be out of copyright, she took sections and sang them on the backing track. After approaching director Jimmy Murakami to make a video for the song, she assumed Joyce's grandson, Stephen James Joyce, must have the rights to the book and contacted him several times, over more than a year, for permission to use the passages, but in vain. In the end, she kept the backing track but wrote her own lyric that sounded close to the original prose while adding a new dimension, of *'stepping out of the page into the sensual world'*, or of Molly Bloom stepping out of the book and walking into real life. She also referred to William Blake's *Jerusalem*: 'And my arrows of desire rewrite the speech'.

One of the main hooks in the chorus was inspired by a traditional Macedonian piece, 'Nevestinsko Oro' ('Bride's Dance'), after Kate was sent a recording. As in the time-honoured version, the melody is played on uilleann pipes, by Davy Spillane, with John Sheahan on fiddle and Dónal Lunny on bouzouki, and bass and drums are played by Del Palmer and Charlie Morgan respectively. A fade-in for the first few seconds of pealing church bells also adds an atmospheric touch. Finally, Paddy Bush contributes the sound of whips—or so the credits say. In a fan club newsletter, he begged to put the record straight about 'a mistake made by some silly person who didn't ask'. In fact, he was playing a pair of fishing rods, in order to give the impression of a rich Irish Lakeland, and the swishing sound of the rods was used to conjure up 'the atmosphere of fly-fishing, tweed hats and long Wellingtons'.

Released as a single in 7-inch, 12-inch, cassette, and CD formats on 18 September, a month before the album in Britain, it entered the chart at its peak position of No. 12. On all formats, the bonus track 'Walk Straight Down the

Middle' was included, plus an instrumental version of 'The Sensual World' on all formats except the 7-inch and cassette single. It was also the last of her singles released on 7-inch vinyl in Japan. The British 12-inch had a double-grooved A-side so that either the song or an instrumental version of the song would play, depending on where the stylus was placed. Mastering engineer Ian Cooper said that she arranged this without warning EMI about it, and some 12-inch singles were returned by unsuspecting buyers who thought they had a faulty vocal-free copy. The company therefore had to put a warning sticker on the cover.

The song was re-recorded for *Director's Cut* over twenty years later, after permission from the Joyce estate was finally obtained to use the original text from *Ulysses*, in a new version renamed 'Flower of the Mountain' (see p. 108).

A video, in which Kate danced through an enchanted forest in a medieval dress, was co-directed by Kate with Comic Strip co-creator Peter Richardson.

2. 'Love and Anger' 4.42

Track two was one of the first started for the album—and evidently one of the most troublesome to complete, being two years in the making. Even Kate herself confessed to having trouble understanding what it was trying to say, as it 'had so many different faces'.[2] The basic theme was one of whom a person could or could not confide in when there was something they found it hard to talk about. Once she had written the first verse, 'I'd already set some form of direction, but I couldn't follow through. I didn't know what I wanted to say at all. I guess I was just trying to make a song that was comforting, up tempo, and about how when things get really bad, it's all right really.' A line early in the song about 'a little piece of hope holding us together' plants a note of positivity that ends in the reassurance that 'if it's so deep you don't think you can speak about it, don't ever think that you can't change the past and the future ... just you wait and see, someone will come to help you'.

Musically, too, it was anything but straightforward. Stuart Elliott played drums, John Giblin bass, and Dave Gilmour guitar, but none of them without difficulty: 'It was one of those awful tracks where either everything would sound ordinary, really middle-of-the-road'.[3]

Perseverance won the day, although even after it was released, she still did not regard it as finished. The result was hardly middle-of the road, but a passionate, almost fiercely brisk shuffling number, Gilmour's almost snarling guitar vying with Paddy's valiha, a tube zither made of bamboo from Madagascar, regarded as the national instrument, sometimes used on the island for ritual music to summon spirits.

In Britain EMI chose it as the third single from the album, although it charted only at No. 38. In spite of this, it reached No. 1 on the US Billboard Modern Rock Tracks, her only chart-topper in any form in America. In addition to the standard 7-inch in Britain, a limited edition 7-inch in gatefold sleeve with booklet of photos from the music video supplemented the 12-inch, cassette, and CD singles. All formats included the bonus track 'Ken', and all except the 7-inch and cassette singles had two instrumental tracks, 'One Last Look Around the House Before We Go' and 'The Confrontation'. All three songs were written for the episode 'GLC: The Carnage Continues...' of British TV programme *The Comic Strip*.

A video directed by Kate was basically of a performance, featuring dancers plus an appearance by the KT Bush Band and by David Gilmour.

3. 'The Fog' 5.04

Two main threads run through the inspiration for this song. One is the theme of being in water, as was 'The Ninth Wave', and the other is growing up, which Kate said 'for most people is just trying to stop escaping, looking at things inside yourself rather than outside. But I'm not sure if people ever grow up properly. It's a continual process, growing in a positive sense.'[4]

At the same time, there is the theme of 'a big expanse of water, and being in a relationship now and flashing back to being a child being taught how to swim, and using these two situations as the idea of learning to let go'. It was partly autobiographical for her—the old learning curve with a father taking his children into the water, holding them by the hands, and inviting them to swim towards him as he walked backwards little. The gap may be getting bigger, but they know their father will not let them drown. The swimming is therefore an analogy for learning and growing.[5] In the first few seconds, her father's voice can be heard, instructing her to put her feet down.

Writing the song began at the Fairlight with 'these big chords of strings', a line over the top, and then the idea of words about slipping into the fog. She thought it would be interesting to visualise that in a piece of music, with strings coming in that would actually be the fog. The music gradually developed, 'then went into the big orchestral bit, to get the sense of fog coming in'. Enter Stuart Elliott on drums and Nigel Kennedy replacing the Fairlight violin. 'He's great to work with—such a great musician,' she said. 'The times we work together we sort of write together. I'll say something like, "what about doing something a bit like Vaughan Williams?" and he'll know the whole repertoire, and he'll pick something, and maybe I'll change something.' After that the lyrics flowed easily about 'slipping into the fog, and relationships, trying to let go of people'. Also playing on the track are Alan Murphy on guitar and synth, Jonathan Williams on cello, Alan Stivell or Celtic harp, and Davy Spillane on whistles. What begins as a largely acoustic song soon takes flight into an atmospheric five-minute drama with the violin and cello to the forefront.

The final touch came when they contacted Michael Kamen, who had orchestrated some of the previous album, and was asked if he could supply something suggesting waves and flashbacks. His track record as a writer for films and love of the idea of visual imagery made him ideal for what was required, and his string arrangement was added on top of the Fairlight. It was a complicated process, she admitted. 'I don't know how anything comes out as one song, because sometimes it's such a bizarre process. It does seem to work together somehow.'[6]

4. 'Reaching Out' 3.11

Just when the album had started to become 'all sort of dark and down', and Kate needed another song to lift it, she found inspiration after a walk in the park, following a conversation with someone about a star that exploded. The 'fantastic imagery' immediately appealed to her imagination, leading her to write a number about taking the idea of how people cling on to things that change, often in an effort to prevent things from changing. The image of people reaching up for a star, which then suddenly exploded, appealed to her. It seemed to sum up the whole idea of how a person could not hold on to anything 'because everything is always changing and we all have such a terrible need to hold onto stuff and to keep it exactly how it is, because this is nice and we don't want it to change.' She sat down at the piano and the song came quite easily.

Her vocals alternate according to the intensity of the music behind her, little more than a whisper at some points, close to a passionate wail the next. As well as the usual musicians, Paddy plays mandolin while Michael Nyman contributes an arrangement for strings, using the Balanescu String Quartet. She told him 'it had to have a sense of uplifting, and I really like his stuff—the rawness of his strings. It's a bit like a fuzzbox touch—quite "punk".'[7]

5. 'Heads We're Dancing' 5.17

The subject matter of the album came no darker than this. It had started with Kate's recollections of a family friend, some years previously, who had been invited to dinner by others and sat next to a really fascinating man. They spent all night chatting and joking—and next day he found out the man was J. Robert Oppenheimer, credited with inventing the atomic bomb. This friend was horrified, as he really despised what the man stood for. Kate was so intrigued by this idea of the man she knew being so taken by this person until they knew who they were, and then finding it completely changed their attitude. It led her to think—what if somebody met a charming, elegant, well-spoken person who turned out to be the devil in disguise? Supposing a girl was at a very expensive, romantic, exciting ball in 1939, just before the war, and a very charming, very sweet-spoken man, came up to her, threw a coin and said that if the coin landed heads up, they should dance together. A couple of days later, she would glance at the paper, and realise with horror that she had been dancing with Hitler. Had she known what was actually happening, she could have tried to kill him and therefore changed history. While Kate had some qualms in glorifying such a scenario, she knew that in a film, it would be acceptable, although in a song it might be a more sensitive issue.[8]

For her, what made the track so musically distinctive is Mick Karn's fretless bass, which gives such a different feel to the song. She was really impressed with his whole energy on the instrument: 'He's very distinctive—so many people admire him because he stays in that unorthodox area, he doesn't come into the commercial world—he just does his thing'.[9] Also on the track are string players Jonathan Williams on cello and Nigel Kennedy on cello, with the orchestra again arranged by Michael Kamen. Stuart Elliott's drums contribute an almost machine-like beat at the start, taking on a more intense feel as the other instruments enter.

6. 'Deeper Understanding' 4.46

Kate explained that the song was about how people are replacing human relationships with technology, and even more true in the twenty-first century than when she wrote the song. It was the start of the age when more and more people were having less contact with human beings, spending all day on the phone, and all night watching television—when not pressing buttons on Ceefax for their shopping. A long chain of machines was actually stopping people from going out properly into the world, isolating and containing them in their homes. Nowhere was this more relevant than in the case of people living in London in high-rise flats who did not know their neighbours, or anyone else in the building. People were getting very isolated, had less and less human contact, but more and more contact with their computer, often working on it all day and all night.

People were really building up 'heavy relationships with their computers', she said. Then somebody sees an advertisement in a magazine for a new program for lonely and lost people. They send off for it, receive it, load it up in their computer and then 'it turns into this big voice that's saying to them, "Look, I know that you're not very happy, and I can offer you love: I'm here to love you. I love you!" And it's the idea of a divine energy coming through the least expected thing. For me, when I think of computers, it's such a cold contact and yet, at the same time, I really believe that computers could be a tremendous way for us to look at ourselves in a very spiritual way because I think computers could teach us more about ourselves than we've been able to look at, so far.'[10]

There was a positive side to all this. It might be emotional disconnection, she admitted, 'but then it's very much *connection*, but in a way that you would never expect. And that kind of emotion should really come from the human instinctive force, and in this particular case it's coming from a computer.'

She was very taken with the concept of playing with the whole imagery of computers being cold and unfeeling, and writing a song about a person who conjures up a program that seems almost like a sudden arrival of angelic figures. 'They are suddenly given so much love by this computer—it's like, you know, just love. There was no other choice. Who else could embody the visitation of angels but the Trio Bulgarka?'[11]

Apart from the trio's vocals, most of the song's instrumentation comes (appropriately) from keyboards, supplemented by Charlie Morgan on drums, John Giblin on bass, and Paddy Bush on tupan, a large drum used extensively in Middle Eastern music.

7. 'Between a Man and a Woman' 3.29

As Kate observed, is a very finely balanced thing that can be easily thrown off by a third party. The idea for this song came from a line in *The Godfather,* during a family argument, when Marlon Brando said, 'Don't interfere, it's between a man and a woman'.[12] Sometimes a person has the choice, whether to leap in and take over and control—or not.[13]

Musically, it starts with getting a groove going at the piano, and a straightforward Fairlight pattern. Once Stuart Elliott came in on drums, she thought that maybe it was taking on a slightly '60s feel, so Alan Murphy was brought in to add guitar, while Alan Stivell also contributed Celtic harp and backing vocals. She wanted to work with Jonathan Williams on cello again, as she considered it such a beautiful instrument —'very male and female—not one or the other,' she said, adding that he was the only player that she had ever written out music for. Most of her musicians could consider themselves lucky if they were just supplied with a chord chart. As for how the music developed, it came from her and the other musicians 'just playing around with a groove'. As they had a second verse that was similar to the first, her first reaction was that it seemed really dull, and she left it on one side for about six months. After that, she made some modifications that proved just having that little bit on the front worked much better: 'Quite often I have to put things aside and think about them if they just haven't worked. If you leave a little time, it's surprising how often you can come back and turn it into something'.[14]

8. 'Never Be Mine' 3.43

The inspiration for this song, said Kate, came through the idea of how people sometimes find that 'it's the dream you want, not the real thing ... pursuing a conscious realisation that a person is really enjoying the fantasy and aware it won't become reality. So often you think it's the end you want, but this is actually looking at the process that will never get you there. Bit of a heart-game you play with yourself'.[15]

Musically, she felt it called for an eastern sounding rhythm. She wrote it first on the piano to a Fairlight rhythm that Del had programmed, though the words were completely different, except for the choruses. It was based mainly on the tabla at first. Eberhard Weber was asked to play bass, and when they were trying to piece the result together later it lacked the feel she was looking for, 'so we just took the bass out and had it in these two sections'. The end result was a song that had 'a very light feel about it, which helps the whole imagery. The Uillean pipes have a very light feel, and the piano is light'. They used an upright Bernstein piano with 'a really nice sound', having initially tried using a large piano in a small room, 'and it didn't record well. The small piano sounds much bigger'.[16] As well as Davey Spillane on pipes, the Trio Bulgarka again sang backing vocals, with musician and singers combining in unison to marvellous effect during the chorus.

9. 'Rocket's Tail' 4.06

One of Kate's cats, Rocket, helped to provide the subject matter. In typically enigmatic fashion, she said the song was not exactly about him, but 'kind of inspired by him and for him, but the song, it's about anything'. Blink and you miss it, in fact—an ephemeral, fleeting moment to be savoured before it was gone:

> I guess it's saying there's nothing wrong with being right here at this moment, and just enjoying this moment to its absolute fullest, and if that's it, that's OK, you know. And it's kind of using the idea of a rocket that's so exciting for maybe three seconds and then it's gone, you know that's it, but so what, it had three seconds of absolutely wonderful.

More than any of the other songs on the album, this was written with the Trio Bulgarka in mind, as she wanted one that would really showcase their vocal skills. The other two on the album on which they appeared were already structured, and in a way the singers' contributions had to fit neatly around the pattern of each to become a part of it, while this one was based around them. She wrote it on a synthesizer with a choir sound and simply sang along.[17]

In order to have their voices in as dominant a way as possible, she put the basic track down with a DX7 choir sound so it had a particular vocal feel, then arranged for Stuart Elliott to get a rock 'n' roll vibe going on the drums. Next she brought some friends in to hear what it would sound like with big block vocals singing behind her voice, and although they were English people that sang completely differently, it still gave her a sense of vocal intensity.

They took it to Bulgaria and started working with an arranger. She told him the effect that she wanted, 'and he just went off and said "what about this?" and they were great'. Having initially decided she wanted the drums to come in near the beginning, she then decided that the first ninety seconds or so needed to be sung *a cappella* with the haunting vocal tapestries behind. It proved an effective contrast with what followed, when 'we let Dave Gilmour rip on it [on guitar], so we'd have this really extreme change from just vocals to this hopefully big Rock'n'Roll kit, with bass, and guitar solos'.[18]

10. 'This Woman's Work' 3.32

This was originally written not for the album, but for the soundtrack of the film *She's Having a Baby*, made the previous year. The lyric was about being forced to confront an unexpected and frightening crisis during the normal event of childbirth. Director John Hughes used it during the film's dramatic climax, when Jake (Kevin Bacon) learned that the lives of his wife (Elizabeth McGovern) and their unborn child were in danger. As the song played, the film showed a montage sequence of flashbacks showing the couple in happier times, intercut with shots of him waiting for news of his wife and their baby's condition.

Kate wrote the song specifically for the sequence, writing from a man's viewpoint, matching the words to the visuals that had already been filmed. She found it one of the quickest songs she had ever written. They had the relevant footage on video, and plugged it up so she could watch the monitor while sitting at the piano and she wrote the song to these visuals. She found there was little more to it than just telling the story, a commission she thoroughly enjoyed.

Released as the album's second single in Britain and reaching No. 25, it was available in 7-inch, 7-inch picture disc, 12-inch (with poster sleeve), cassette, and CD formats. In Germany, a 3-inch CD single was also released. On all formats, the bonus track 'Be Kind to My Mistakes' (see p. 85) was included, plus 'I'm Still Waiting' on all formats except 7-inch and cassette singles.

There were four different versions of the song. The original version was released on the soundtrack album of the film, and that on the album was edited from the original, while the version released as a single was a slightly different mix. A re-recording appeared on *Director's Cut*, simply featuring Kate accompanying herself on piano. The Michael Kamen-arranged strings apart, even the album version has no other musicians apart from Kate herself.

A music video directed by Kate featured her spotlighted in an otherwise black room, playing the introductory notes on a piano. Next, a distraught man (played by Tim McInnerny) paced the waiting room of a hospital, and flashbacks revealed that his wife (played by Kate) had collapsed while they were having dinner. The story then blurred into a continuous scene where he took her to the hospital, his wife being wheeled away on a stretcher as he raced in behind her. While waiting, he imagined the nurse coming to tell him she had died, until she returned to reassure him all was well, followed by a final scene in which she closed the piano keyboard.

It was also subsequently used in an episode of *The Handmaid's Tale*, an American drama television series based on the novel by Margaret Atwood. In 2005, it was featured in the British TV drama *Walk Away and I Stumble*, and after broadcast, it reached No. 3 on the UK download chart. A further lease of life came when it was also used in a long-running UK television advert for the National Society for the Prevention of Cruelty to Children, between 2005 and 2008, and in the Christmas Special of the BBC situation comedy *Extras* in 2007, resulting in another brief appearance in the Top 100.

11. 'Walk Straight Down the Middle' (CD/cassette only) *3.48*

This was another song that Kate found 'came together very quickly'. It was based on an old backing track that she had originally intended as a B-side. She wrote the lyrics and recorded the synth overdubs and vocals in a single day, using the next day for final overdubs and mixing. It was the last track to be finished for the album, created in just over twenty-four hours, with Eberhard Weber on bass and Charlie Morgan on drums the only other musicians used.

Her mother was outside in the garden when 'the funny bits at the end [some interesting vocal bird-like cries] were being played', and she rushed in to tell her excitedly that she had heard peacocks close by. Greatly amused, after explaining what she had done, Kate said that from then on she could no longer take the song seriously. At that point, she had fancied being Captain Beefheart, and the idea just came to her, standing out, calling for help in the middle.

As the title hints, it is about following either of two extremes, when all one wants to do is 'to plough this path straight down the middle'.[19] It was about trying not to get caught in a situation when fear sometimes holds people back from making the right decision, and there is no need to be frightened.

As well as being a bonus track on non-vinyl formats, it was originally released as the B-side of the single of the title track.

In 2013, it appeared on the B-side of the 10-inch single for the recent remix of *Running Up That Hill*.

8

This Woman's Work

A box set released on 22 October 1990, containing the first six albums, plus two additional records of B-sides, rarities and remixes containing a non-album A-side, B-sides, the live tracks from the 1979 EP, and extended remixes. These two discs of collectables were never officially released separately, although some shops bowed to demand and sold them individually.

Tracks—Record 7

1. 'The Empty Bullring 2.13
A slow song recorded solo by Kate at the piano, this concerns someone in love with someone else who is obsessed with something rather futile and who cannot persuade the person to accept the fact. He then becomes a matador, until he is gored so badly that he cannot continue. One night he climbs out of the window and runs off to a bullring, when nobody else is around, so he can fight an imaginary bull. The original Tamlaine, referred to in the first verse, was a girl in a traditional fairy story, locked up in an ivory tower. It was originally the B-side of 'Breathing'.

2. 'Ran Tan Waltz' 2.39
Here is a semi-comic tale in which the traditional gender roles are turned around. Described by one admirer as a 'Brecht-meets-Irish ballad', it concerns a young husband and father who has been left at home, much to his annoyance, looking after the baby while his wife is out, getting drunk, having affairs, and paying no attention to the family. 'I'm holding the baby, she's ran-tanning constantly,' he grumbles (she sings) in the refrain.

What could have been a rather pathetic tale is sung with humour, underlined when Kate performed it during the 1979 Christmas Special *Kate* with two dancers, she being dressed as the put-upon spouse and father, complete with a scruffy false beard. Released a few months later as the B-side of 'Babooshka', it would be the first of several non-album tracks to appear on singles.

3. 'Passing Through Air' 2.01

The earliest of Kate's recordings to be released officially, this was taped as a demo in 1973, a few weeks after her fifteenth birthday, at Dave Gilmour's studio, or as the original sleeve credit reads, 'Produced by Dave Gilmour on a sunny afternoon at Dave's'. He played guitar alongside Pat Martin on bass and Pete Perrier on drums. The two latter musicians were part of country rock band Unicorn, who had previously been a backing band for Billy J. Kramer. 'Passing through air, you mix the stars with your arms,' she sings in a short, jaunty love song.

It was first released as one of two tracks on the B-side of 'Army Dreamers' in 1980.

4. 'December Will Be Magic Again' 4.49

Recorded in 1979 and premiered during the Christmas Special that December, this seasonal song was released on 17 November 1980, her first standalone single, reaching No. 29. Her sole contribution to the catalogue of Yuletide hits, an alternate version with bongos and slide whistles on the rhythm track has subsequently appeared on Christmas various artists' compilation albums.

5. 'Warm and Soothing' 2.42

A bittersweet number, again sung by Kate at her piano, the lyrics initially describe a happy family home, and then a horror of eventual old age, while trapped in a relationship that was anything but warm and soothing. Kate was planning to use Abbey Road shortly, and wanted to record one of her songs there with piano and vocal as a sound quality control test. This was the one, tried out in 1980, and the studio indeed measured up to her expectations. It was first released later that year as the B-side of 'December Will Be Magic Again'.

6. 'Lord of the Reedy River' (Donovan Leitch) 2.42

This was the first of several songs written by others that Kate recorded for release. Donovan had composed it in 1968 and issued his version on the album *H.M.S. Donovan* in 1971. By then it had been covered by Mary Hopkin on her first album *Post Card* in 1969, with its writer on guitar and backing vocals, plus Paul McCartney (who produced the album) also on guitar, and also Israeli duo Esther and Abi Ofarim on their 1968 album *Up To Date*. As a long-time admirer of Donovan, Kate had always wanted to cover one of his songs. While she was watching a Crystal Gayle show on TV one evening, somebody asked her what she planned to put on the B-side of her forthcoming single 'Sat in Your Lap', and she said she planned to record this. Suddenly Crystal introduced Donovan as her special guest, and it was the first time she had seen him on television for several years.

When she came to do so, she wanted to sound as if she was floating down a river while she was singing. She therefore went to a disused swimming pool in the basement of Townhouse Studios, so her voice could be recorded reflecting off the water. To her delight, she said, Donovan came into the studio to provide backing vocals, a dream come true for her as she had always wanted to work with him. How much of his contribution survives is another matter. A careful listen to the song suggests that she is singing unaccompanied except for a delicate pan pipes-like instrument perhaps sampled through a Fairlight, plus towards the end a male voice—maybe his—whispering a couple of hard-to-decipher words while she sings the closing line.

The song tells of the myth of Leda and the Swan, the former being a girl who falls in love with a swan and is changed into one.

7. 'Ne T'Enfuis Pas' (Kate Bush, French lyrics by Patrick Jeaneau and Vivienne Chandler) 2.10

In translation, 'Don't Run Away', this tells the story of a woman who is worried that her lover might leave, wrestling with her conscience over her plans to make him stay. It was originally released as the B-side of 'There Goes a Tenner' in Britain, and 'Suspended in Gaffa' in Europe. In both cases, the title was misspelled as 'Ne T'en Fuis Pas'. Kate is featured on Fairlight as well as vocals, and Del Palmer on a basic backing of fretless bass and Linn drum programming.

It also appeared as a single in July 1983 in France and Canada, featuring 'Un Baiser d'Enfant' on the B-side.

8. 'Un Baiser d'Enfant' (Kate Bush, French lyrics by François Cahan) 3.00

A French version of 'The Infant Kiss' (see p. 41), this simple delicate ballad was recorded in October 1982 in one day by Kate, with Del Palmer and Paul Hardiman engineering. Alan Murphy plays electric guitar, with strings provided by Adam and Jo Skeaping.

It was the B-side of 'Ne T'Enfuis Pas', as well as appearing on the Canadian/USA mini-LP *Kate Bush*, in remixed form featuring cleaner-sounding vocals.

9. 'Under the Ivy' 2.06
A breathtakingly simple song featuring just Kate and her piano, this was one of several songs recorded during the sessions for *Hounds of Love*. It is a wistful,

contemplative number about lost innocence, recalling magical moments from childhood, and a longing to be completely alone for a while—'This little girl inside me is retreating to her favourite place, go into the garden, go under the ivy, under the leaves, away from the party'.

It was originally released as the B-side of 'Running Up That Hill' in 1985. She performed it once on TV, singing and playing the grand piano at Abbey Road Studios in London, for the 100th episode of Channel 4's *The Tube* in March 1986.

10. 'Burning Bridge' 4.44

Kate succinctly called it 'just a positive and trivial song, with superficial lyrics'. It was also included in the 1997 'EMI Centenary' re-release of *Hounds of Love*. As it was created specifically for a B-side, she felt it needed to be something that would counterbalance the energy of the other side. A relatively up-tempo 'fun song' was therefore called for. Its lyrics about 'crossing the bridge, the burning bridge, with flames behind us', and 'you and me, babe, against the world', may not be her most weighty, but with a strong simple beat and catchy refrain, the number always remained one of her most infectious cuts.

It first appeared as the B-side of 'Cloudbusting' in 1985.

11. 'My Lagan Love' (traditional, new lyrics by Kate Bush) 2.29

A traditional Irish air collected in 1903 in northern Donegal, and recorded by many others including John McCormack, Van Morrison with The Chieftains, Sinead O'Connor, and Barbara Dickson, for which Kate wrote new original lyrics and sings *a cappella*. The Lagan of the title is assumed to be the river running through Belfast.

It was first released in 1985 as the second B-side track on the 12-inch version of 'Cloudbusting', and also included in the 1997 'EMI Centenary' re-release of *Hounds of Love*.

12. 'The Handsome Cabin Boy' 3.11

Another old traditional song (although credited on the label to Kate Bush herself), this had been recorded by many others, among them Ewan MacColl and A. L. Lloyd, Martin Carthy, and as 'The Handsome Cabin Boy Waltz', by Jerry Garcia of Grateful Dead and David Grisman, with the sole accompaniment being a one-note ethereal backing vocal behind her voice. She omits two verses, which in the view of some listeners thus failed to tell the full story—namely that of a pretty young girl who dresses herself as a sailor, goes to sea, and befriends the captain, but her deception is eventually unmasked.

It was recorded during sessions for *Hounds of Love,* released as the B-side of the title track as a single in 1986, and also included in the 1997 'EMI Centenary' re-release of *Hounds*.

13. 'Not This Time' 3.39

A slow, brooding number, this comes close to AOR power ballad territory, the type of material in which acts like Heart and Pat Benatar specialised at the time. Over a dramatic backing of piano, organ and plaintive guitar, with backing vocals rising to a crescendo towards the end, she delivered a passionate song declaring that she does not know why she gives in, 'but I do every time, and here I am wondering why I did it again.' As the chorus lyrics read, it has got to end: 'I fear you, and I forget myself, but not this time'.

Recorded during sessions for *Hounds of Love* in 1984, this was released as the B-side of 'The Big Sky' two years later.

14. 'Walk Straight Down the Middle' 3.51

15. 'Be Kind to My Mistakes' 2.59

Kate was offered the female lead in Nicolas Roeg's 1986 film *Castaway*, starring Oliver Reed, but turned it down. Fans were thus denied the chance of seeing rather more of her than usual, and the role went to Amanda Donohoe instead. Nevertheless she wrote this song, featured over the opening credits. The title was spoken by Oliver Reed's character at the end of the film. A punchy, up-tempo number, it derives a certain amount of energy from the brisk guitar and backing vocals.

Its first appearance on record was on the original motion picture soundtrack album, released in 1987 on LP only, followed by a German-only promotional 7-inch single, with 'Chemistry' by Brian Eno, also from the soundtrack. There are three versions: the original, on the soundtrack, the one on the promotional 7-inch single, and a remix on the B-side of the single 'This Woman's Work' as well as on this collection and on the American and Canadian mini-album *Aspects of the Sensual World*. The original version has a longer intro than the 1989 remix and a slightly different ending, with more echo on percussion. The version on the promotional 7-inch single fades out, where the album version on the soundtrack crossfades into the next track.

Tracks—Record 8

1. 'I'm Still Waiting' 4.31

Unconnected with a 1971 Diana Ross song of the same title, this was originally released on the 12-inch and CD singles of 'This Woman's Work' in 1989, and on *Aspects of the Sensual World* in 1990. A lyric of yearning looks to a better future ahead in an unsettled relationship: 'Maybe the love has gone, but there's still a heart that's beating, though the clouds have come, maybe the sun will come out … maybe you'll be coming back, 'cause I'm still waiting.' Sung at a fairly brisk pace, with her keyboards, backing vocals and electronic drums, it is one of her more commercial numbers.

2. 'Ken' 3.47

Written and recorded for a sketch in a 1990 episode of TV series *The Comic Strip*, about the then Labour member of parliament and former leader of the Greater London Council, Ken Livingstone, the lyrics included: 'Look to the left and to the right, we need help and there's nobody in sight, where is the man that we all need? Well tell him he's to come and rescue me, Ken is the man that we all need, Ken is the leader of the GLC.' Musically it sounds not a million miles removed from Prince's '1999' with its dance vibe and stabs of keyboard chords. The general feel and a line in the call-and-respond section 'Who is the funky sex machine? KEN!' suggests a light-hearted throwaway effort that may have been intended affectionately, satirically, or a mixture of both. Despite the heartfelt anti-war tone of two of her singles released in 1980, shortly after the election of a Conservative government in Britain, Kate rarely spoke to the press about politics or politicians, a notable exception being in 2015 when her remarks about the later Conservative Prime Minister Theresa May were selectively quoted out of context, and she later felt impelled to issue a statement affirming that she was not a Tory supporter.

It was released as the B-side of the single 'Love and Anger' in 1990, and included on the cassette, 12-inch single, and CD singles, and on *Aspects of the Sensual World*.

In March 2014, Livingstone, who subsequently served as Labour mayor of London from 2000 to 2008, proudly told David Mellor, former Conservative cabinet minister turned presenter, on an LBC (London Broadcasting) radio show that Kate had written a song about him. Referring to her forthcoming concerts, he said he did not know whether listeners would be applying for tickets, 'but don't forget, she did *one great song*—Ken Is The Leader Of The GLC—which I've still got at home. It's very good' (present author's italics).[1]

3. 'One Last Look Around the House Before We Go' 1.00

Sixty seconds of delicate melody on the piano comprise this instrumental fragment. First heard on the soundtrack of *The Comic Strip*'s 'GLC', it was later released on the 12-inch and CD formats of 'Love and Anger'.

4. 'Wuthering Heights (new vocal)' 5.02

5. 'Experiment IV' 4.19

6. 'Them Heavy People' (live) 4.10

7. *'Don't Push Your Foot on the Heartbreak' (live) 3.39*

8. *'James and the Cold Gun' (live) 6.18*

9. *'L'Amour Looks Something Like You' (live) 2.47*
Tracks 6–9 were from the 1979 *On Stage* EP, recorded at Hammersmith Odeon on the Tour of Life, 13 May 1979. All except 'L'Amour' were also included on *Live at Hammersmith Odeon*, issued as a video in 1981 and again in a boxed set in 1994 with CD, 'James and the Cold Gun' being over two minutes longer (see pp. 25, 27).

10. *'Running Up That Hill (A Deal With God)' 5.42*

11. *'Cloudbusting' (The Organon Mix) 6.36*
About ninety seconds longer than the 7-inch single, this starts with forty seconds of powerful drumming and has a longer final section, plus additional echo effects along the way.

12. *'Hounds of Love' (Alternative) 3.51*
Replacing the spoken sampled dialogue at the start is an intro of about thirty seconds of Fairlight strings and percussion, but thereafter there is little difference between this and the better-known version.

13. *'The Big Sky' (Meteorological Mix) 8.03*
Again, the major difference between the 7-inch single and its big brother is in the intro, just over a minute of sampled sounds on the Fairlight, dominated by percussion that gradually takes on the intensity of tribal drum sounds, leading into an extended busy vocal section with lengthy fade.

14. *'Experiment IV' (12-inch mix) 6.48*
Once more, the extended mix opens with a longer intro with Nigel Kennedy's eerie violin, then Fairlight drums to the fore, both taking centre stage for about two minutes. Ninety seconds of instrumentation about halfway through act as a bridge for both vocal sections.

9

The Red Shoes

UK:	Released 2 November 1993, EMI, No. 2
US:	Released 1993, Columbia, No. 28
Current edition:	CD
Personnel:	Kate Bush: vocals, keyboards (except 4), piano (4, 5, 8, 9), Fender Rhodes (5, 8, 12), bass guitar and guitar (10)
	Del Palmer: Fairlight programming, electronic drums
	Stuart Elliott: drums (1–3, 6–9, 11, 12), percussion (1, 3, 5, 7)
	John Giblin: bass guitar (1–3, 6, 8, 9, 12)
	Danny McIntosh: guitar (1, 5–9)
	Horn section (1, 3, 9, 11):
	Nigel Hitchcock: tenor and baritone saxophone (1)
	Steve Sidwell: trumpet, flugelhorn (11)
	Paul Spong: trumpet
	Neil Sidwell: trombone
	Gary Brooker: Hammond organ (2, 9, 12)
	Eric Clapton: guitar (2)
	Paddy Bush: vocals (3, 7, 9), valiha, singing bowls and fujara (6), musical bow, whistle and mandola (7)
	Justin Vali: valiha (3, 7), kabosy and vocals (3)
	Trio Bulgarka: vocals (5, 11, 12)
	Dimitar Penev: vocal arrangements for Trio Bulgarka
	Charlie Morgan: percussion (5)
	Lily Cornford: narrator (6)
	Colin Lloyd Tucker: vocals (7, 9)
	Gaumont d'Olivera: bass guitar (7), drums, percussion and sound effects (10)
	Nigel Kennedy: violin (8, 10), viola (8)
	Prince: keyboards, guitar, bass guitar, vocals and co-arranger (11)

Lenny Henry: vocals (11)
Jeff Beck: guitar (12)
Recorded at Abbey Road, London, 1991–3
Produced by Kate Bush

This, the first album where Kate's face did not appear on the outer sleeve, would be her last record for twelve years. The song from which it took its name was inspired by the 1948 film of the same name by Michael Powell and Emeric Pressburger, in turn inspired by Hans Christian Andersen's fairy tale concerning a dancer, possessed by her art, who cannot take off the shoes and find peace. When she began writing new material in the summer of 1990, it was with the intention of creating something with greater simplicity, feeling that previously her music had often been too complicated or 'arty' for people to absorb and she now wanted to make it more of 'an easy experience'.

Intending to go out on tour immediately after it was released, she deliberately aimed for a more live feel on record with less studio embellishments, thus marking a break with the three previous albums. Del Palmer confirmed in an interview that the intention was to record it quickly so they could take it out on the road. Although that never happened, the idea influenced the way it was put together. For the first time in years, several of the songs were built upon the sound on a bass guitarist and drummer, John Giblin and Stuart Elliott respectively, playing together in the same room. More importantly, the Fairlight that had dominated the previous few albums was put aside after the original demos had been recorded, in favour of more conventional keyboards.

During the recording of the album, although after the songs had been written, 'several unhappy things were occurring'. Just over two years, she lost guitarist Alan Murphy in October 1989 and one of her dance partners, Gary Hurst, the following year, both from AIDS, and most importantly of all her mother, Hannah, who succumbed to cancer in February 1992. Devastated, she admitted later that as a result she had no desire to sing or even work for several months. Her long-term personal relationship with bassist Del Palmer also ended at around this time, although when she resumed recording, they continued to work together. Nevertheless a new major presence in her life arrived in the shape of Danny McIntosh, formerly guitarist with '70s group Bandit alongside future solo hitmaker Jim Diamond. An old friend of Del, Brian Bath, and Alan Murphy, he not only filled the huge gap left by the latter but also became Kate's personal partner.

The album featured many more high-profile cameo appearances than before, notably contributions from Lenny Henry, Prince, Eric Clapton, Gary Brooker, and Jeff Beck. Once again, Trio Bulgarka, who were becoming regular guests on her albums, appeared on three songs. It also marked Kate's move from analogue to digital recording, a factor that in the views of some left it sounding tinny, rather than deep and arm like its predecessors. In time she came to agree with the verdict, and in her 2011 album *Director's Cut*, she re-recorded seven of the songs (see p. 107ff).

Having lost any desire to tour, towards the end of the recording sessions she decided to make a film, *The Line, the Cross and the Curve*, featuring six of the songs linked by a narrative theme. Reviews were less than favourable, and she admitted to her disappointment with the result.

While favourably received, the album is generally seen as not her best, and clearly to some extent a reflection of the troubled time she was going through. Despite this, some hold the view that it still manages to be an upbeat collection, in that the songs have a common thread of being brave, strong, and open, having to make a choice between holding on or letting go, and trusting in arriving victorious again on the other side. With the benefit of a quarter of a century's hindsight, it is almost indisputably the most mainstream album to which she ever put her name. Whether this is praise or criticism is for the individual listener to decide.

Tracks

1. 'Rubberband Girl' 4.45

A reflection of Kate's desire for more simplicity in some of her music is reflected in the opening track. The lyrics may not be her most profound, but they demonstrate a happy-go-lucky spirit, 'a rubberband bouncing back to life' after grieving for her loved ones, learning by example from 'those trees [that] bend in the wind, I feel they've got a lot more sense than me, you see I try to resist.' The lesson is evidently not to resist. It was one of the most infectious, straightforward songs she had written and recorded, even if a little out of character. In retrospect, she admitted that she just wanted to do something really different. It was her least favourite number on the album, and she had considered taking it off, as it did not feel quite as interesting as the others: 'But I thought, at the same time, it was just a bit of fun ... just a silly pop song really'.[1]

It was indeed—but in the best possible sense. Any disc jockey looking desperately for a no-nonsense Kate Bush 'pop' single with which to fill a dancefloor need have looked no further. Its spontaneous groove, which sits happily on one chord almost throughout yet never becoming monotonous, has the hallmarks of a song written partly if not wholly in the studio instead of being painstakingly honed to perfection long before recording. Colin Lloyd-Tucker, who sang backing vocals on a couple of other tracks (and later recorded an album with Paddy Bush), recalled that in its early stages it was still very rough with hardly anything on it but a guide vocal: 'She was still working out the lyrics—she had a verse, which she kept repeating on the rough version, and said she was going to do the words later'.[2] 'Here I go—yeah', she interjects at one point not far from the end. It suggests that for once she and the band—Stuart Elliott on drums and percussion, John Giblin on bass, Danny McIntosh on guitar, and a brass section comprising Nigel Hitchcock on tenor and baritone saxes, Neil Sidwell on trombone, plus Paul Spong and Steve Sidwell on trumpets—are having fun improvising and simply going with the flow.

The first of four British singles from the album (and, excluding 'Rocket Man', her first new release for over three years), it was released in the UK on 6 September 1993, entering at its peak position of No. 12, and in the USA, on 7 December, where it reached No. 88. In the UK, it was a 7-inch single, a 12-inch single picture disc, a cassette single, and a CD single. All formats featured the B-side 'Big Stripey Lie', with an extended mix of lead track and 'Rubberband Girl' on the 12-inch single and some CD singles, an extended mix of appeared. In the US, the single was on CD only, with the non-album track 'Show a Little Devotion'.

In addition to the version used on the album and single version and an extended one, both released in September, a year later, a 'U.S. remix', by American DJ Eric Kupper, appeared as an extra track on the single release of 'And So Is Love', and in 2011, a re-recording on *Director's Cut*.

Of the two different music videos the original, also used in *The Line, The Cross and The Curve*, features Kate dancing in a studio, while a different one was made for America with her wearing sunglasses and singing the track, intercut with scenes from the film.

2. 'And So Is Love' 4.18

After a lively start, the album enters more sombre territory with a soul-baring, relatively confessional song. The subject is a smooth, tasteful number on the situation between two lovers nearing the end of the road, and realising they have to let go. The listener might be forgiven for thinking it was an epitaph for Kate's personal relationship with Del.

By her normal standards, this is a relatively conventional piece of work, due in part perhaps to the presence of two heavyweight names. Gary Brooker's Hammond organ lays down a wonderful sheen, while Eric Clapton's relaxed guitar phrases curl around between the vocal lines. Although they added their contributions separately and were not in the studio together, it was an appropriate pairing, as both had worked with each other regularly in concerts and on sessions over the last few years and would continue to do so, most famously at the all-star George Harrison tribute show in November 2002. When Eric arrived at the studio, his guitar technician brought along a van full of equipment. Del told him that what they wanted was his 'classic' sound, he plugged in one of his smallest amps and completed the work at once. Poignantly, he did so only two months after the devastating loss of his little son Conor. Del was full of admiration for his honouring the commitment at such a time; he 'only really plays in one style, but he's a genius at what he does'.[3]

Released as the album's fourth single in the UK on 7 November 1994, over a year after the album, it entered at No. 26 in the UK singles chart and resulted in her first appearance on BBC's *Top of the Pops* for nine years, a lip-synching performance accompanied by two female backing singers. It was available as a picture disc 7-inch single with large poster and as two CD singles, one in regular small case, one in large case with three 5-inch by 5-inch card prints. All also included the US mix of 'Rubberband Girl, while the two CD singles also featured the US mix of 'Eat the Music'.

The music video featured in *The Line, The Cross and The Curve* features Kate singing the song in a dark room lit only by a candle.

3. 'Eat the Music' 5.11

A second comparatively playful and carefree number, this has a sunny Caribbean feel, as Kate sings on the joys of food and love metaphors. 'Let's split him open, like a pomegranate, insides out, all is revealed,' she sings. She said she wanted it to feel joyous and sunny, and she just had to provide the fruit. Some critics and listeners found it a joke that soon wore thin, but although musically it might veer dangerously close to novelty or even a throwaway tune from someone capable of far better, it certainly sounds like an exuberant record that was fun to make. On a deeper level, it can be taken as being about opening up in relationships to reveal who we really are inside.

Much of the flavour (excuse pun) comes from Malagasy musician Justin Vali, who played valiha (zither) and kabosy (box-shaped guitar). Kate had met him through her brother, Paddy, who was also featured on valiha and backing vocals, alongside the usual rhythm and brass section.

It was the first single from the album released in the US on 7 September 1993. As the plan had been to do likewise in Britain, a few 7-inch and promotional CD singles were produced and then recalled, indicating a late change of plan. A few other countries, including Australia and the Netherlands, had a summer 1994 release.

The US CD single featured the album version and 12-inch version, with 'Big Stripey Lie' and 'Candle in the Wind'. A two-track CD single released in the Netherlands in the summer of 1994 featured 'Eat the Music' and 'You Want Alchemy'. The Dutch and Australian four-track CD singles featured these two tracks plus the 12-inch 4.55 American edit, and 'Shoedance (The Red Shoes Dance Mix)'. The Australian CD single came in a 'Scratch and Sniff' card sleeve.

There are four versions: the five-minute eleven-second album version, the four-minute fifty-five-second American CD single edit, a three-minute twenty-five-second 'edit radio', released on a French promotional CD-single, and an additional US 12-inch remix, the longest at nine minutes and twenty-one seconds.

The music video, used in *The Line, The Cross and The Curve*, features Kate in a field of fruits with other dancers.

4. 'Moments of Pleasure' 5.18

If two of the first three tracks on the album sounded lightweight or shallow to some, the next redressed the balance in style. Her most heartfelt and poignant song to date, it is ushered in with delicate piano, suddenly all but swept away in Michael Kamen's stirring orchestral arrangement. Her voice likewise follows the changes, starting with almost a whisper to something stronger, until her anguished cry on the chorus sounds like a refusal to be overwhelmed by grief: 'Just being alive, it can really hurt, and these moments are a gift from time'. At the end comes a tribute to those she had lost: Alan Murphy, Bill Duffield, and 'Teddy', former Abbey Road Studios engineer John Barrett, who had worked on *Never For Ever* and *The Dreaming*, although already stricken with the cancer that claimed him in 1984, and director Michael Powell, with whom she had discussed working in the future shortly before his death in 1990.

It plays out like the closing credits of an old-fashioned film. Just as heartfelt is the old conversation she had with her mother, Hannah, who was ill while Kate was writing the song. Yet to call it a sad song is missing the point, as Kate herself said nearly twenty years later. She had included a favourite phrase of her mother's, 'every old sock meets an old shoe', and when she recorded the number and played it to her mother, the latter found it hilarious: 'She couldn't stop laughing, she just thought it was so funny that I'd put it into this song. So I don't see it as a sad song. I think there's a sort of reflective quality, but I guess I think of it more as a celebration of life'.[4] In an earlier verse, she sings about 'The case of George the Wipe! Oh God I can't stop laughing'. This refers to a tape operator at Townhouse Studios who in 1981 inadvertently erased one of the songs recorded for *The Dreaming*. Immediately she followed it with the observation that 'this sense of humour of mine, it isn't funny at all'.

Released as the album's second single on 15 November 1993, it reached No. 26. Several different formats were available: cassette single, 12-inch single with poster, regular CD single, and limited edition box set CD-single with card prints. Limited 7-inch vinyl copies were pressed only for promotional purposes and jukeboxes. The 7-inch and cassette singles featured an instrumental version on the B-side, while the 12-inch single added 'Home for

Christmas'. The CD singles also included 'December Will Be Magic Again' and 'Experiment IV', while a non-limited version added 'Show a Little Devotion'. A Dutch two-track CD single featured 'Home for Christmas' as the second track.

The music video in *The Line, The Cross and The Curve* features Kate in the snow, lip-synching the song and meeting various actors near the end.

She premiered the song during an appearance on BBC TV in *Aspel & Co.* on 20 June 1993, interviewed by Michael Aspel and then performing the song on stage, sitting at a black grand piano.

5. 'The Song of Solomon' 4.29

An old literary text meets human desire in this song in the same way that 'The Sensual World' allows Molly Bloom in *Ulysses* to step off the page and experience her own physical pleasure. In this case, no copyright considerations prevented Kate from taking lines from the Hebrew Bible. To these, she added a chorus of yearning: 'Don't want your bullshit, yeah, just want your sexuality'. A slow, brooding and almost ambient song, despite the presence of the Trio Bulgarka on backing vocals it somehow fails to catch fire.

6. 'Lily' 3.53

Lily Cornford was a renowned spiritual healer in London with whom Kate became close friends in the 1990s. She believed strongly in mental colour healing, a process that enabled her patients to be cured of their ills by seeing various different hues. Kate called her 'one of those very rare people who are intelligent, intuitive and kind', and was so impressed with her strength and knowledge that she decided to celebrate her in song—something the surprised subject found 'hilarious'.

Lily's own narration of The Gayatri, a Hindu mantra, takes up the first forty seconds, then giving way to a bustling, almost hip-hop beat, played live by the band in the studio. Paddy Bush, who could always be relied on to add some exotic instrument, plays fujare (a large folk shepherd's flute from Slovakia), and singing bowls.

Kate's vocal undergoes several changes, from a yearning in the verse, a deep-voiced spoken part in the bridge, a strong call-out during the chorus. 'I said "Lily, oh Lily, I'm so afraid, I fear I am walking in the vale of darkness,"' she sings.

It was also performed live as the opening song during her *Before the Dawn* shows.

7. 'The Red Shoes' 4.03

The title track tells the story of the girl who donned the red leather ballet shoes that had a mind of her own and made her dance a frantic Irish jig. It is another great excuse, if any is needed, for more Celtic sounds, supplied by Paddy Bush's mandola, whistles, and musical bow, and Justin Vali's valiha, to mention nothing of the magic of old classic stories. Once again, Kate elegantly combines a shrill, possessed vocal and a song with an infectious tune that hovers around and barely strays from one chord throughout, with elements of world music.

Released as a single in the UK on 4 April 1994, it reached No. 21. It was the lead track of the movie *The Line, The Cross and The Curve*, presented on film festival at the time of the single's release. It was available as a 7-inch, cassette, and two different CD singles. The 7-inch and cassette both featured on-album track 'You Want Alchemy' on the B-side, while CD single 1 included 'Cloudbusting (Video Mix)' and 'This Woman's Work', and CD single 2, released one week after the other formats, provided 'Shoedance', a ten-minute remix by Karl Blagan of 'The Red Shoes', featuring excerpts from dialogue from *The Line, The Cross & The Curve* with the single remix of 'The Big Sky' and the 12-inch version of 'Running Up That Hill'.

8. 'Top of the City' 4.15
This explores similar subject matter to 'And So Is Love', the tale of a woman sitting up in the skies, looking down on a lonely city below while she sought an answer. 'I don't know if I'm closer to Heaven, but it looks like Hell down there,' she sings, caught between exhilaration, melancholy and desperation. 'I don't know if you'll love me for it, but I don't think we should suffer for this, there's just one thing we can do about it.'

Some passages of the song are very subdued, with just Kate's piano behind her vocal, contrasting with others as her voice soars, with the celestial sounds of the Trio Bulgarka behind her, and occasional bursts of violin and viola courtesy of Nigel Kennedy. One of the less highly-regarded numbers on the album, biographer Rob Jovanovic calls it 'Kate-Bush-by-numbers, a tune she could probably turn out in her sleep'.[5]

9. 'Constellation of the Heart' 4.47
Undoubtedly the funkiest song on the album with something of a Prince flavour, this features a busy froth of guitars, organs and brass section, plus call-and-respond vocals between Kate, Paddy Bush, and Colin Lloyd-Tucker. The first line refers to '[taking] all the telescopes', turning them inside out and pointing them away from the big sky—a reference to her earlier song—as we tend to the universe within ourselves, the constellation of the heart. It has a message of hope in that there is no gain without pain: 'Who said anything about it hurting, it's gonna be beautiful, it's gonna be wonderful, it's gonna be paradise, just being alive, it can really hurt'.

10. 'Big Stripey Lie' 3.33

The last song to be written for the album and one of her most enigmatic, Thomson calls it 'engagingly odd if ultimately unconvincing', while to Jovanovic it is 'an odd beast, not really sure where it should be going'.[6,7] Its imagery conjures up a mood of chaos, despair, fear, of 'all young gentle dreams drowning'. What was the big stripey lie of the title and the first line? It has been suggested that this was a relationship, its metaphor being a predatory animal—a striped tiger, maybe—in the jungle, skulking unseen in the undergrowth. 'Oh my God, it's a jungle in here,' she sang near the end, 'you've got wild animals loose in here.' Nevertheless, there is optimism, or a way out, in her offers to extend a helping hand: 'Can you hang on to me ... Only want to help you, Never want to hurt you, I know I could be good for you'.

To match the somewhat discordant theme, it has a musical setting verging on the discordant. There are no ethereal strings, apart from Nigel Kennedy's violin which rarely if ever aimed to sound ethereal, and it presented Kate playing not only keyboards but also—for the first and so far only time on record—lead and bass guitars (for three minutes, Kate Bush goes grunge). She told Danny that she would love to be able to play the guitar, so he handed her a Fender Telecaster and showed her a few chords. Within a few days, she was in the studio, in front of a Marshall stack, giving it everything as if she was an old hand on the instrument. Whereas the rest of the album was recorded with a band-orientated approach in the studio, this song was created one track at a time. Neither Danny nor Del played on it, the latter calling it 'a sort of stocking filler track ... a sort of Captain Beefheart impersonation on the bass and guitar'.[8] Apart from Kate and Nigel Kennedy, the only musician featured is Gaumont d'Oliveira on drums, percussion, and sound effects.

It also appeared as the B-side of 'Rubberband Girl'.

11. 'Why Should I Love You?' 5.02

Kate went to see Prince at one of his shows at Earl's Court, London, in June 1992. He heard that she was at the show and afterwards sent her a note to say how much he admired her work. She wanted him to record backing vocals for the track that she had recorded at Abbey Road Studios (Studio Number One), but he did not have time to stay in England any longer, so she sent him the tape for him to add them when he was back at his Paisley Park Studios. Presented with the chance to recreate it in his own image, he took it apart and added vocals, guitars, keyboards, drums, and brass. When Kate and Del listened to the result, they were somewhat bemused. Prince's engineer Michael Koppelman was less flattering, calling it 'lame disco'. They worked on it on and off for two years to try to turn it back into the song it had been, to the point of reconstructing it so that it worked with her lyrics. Del even took the original drums and replaced them with a new drum track to match the more upbeat work that Prince had turned it into.

In view of the fact that it was built piece by piece, by two separate teams of collaborators on opposite sides of the Atlantic doing their own thing without consulting each other, the result is surprisingly good—though one could hardly expect otherwise with two such major talents, albeit with their own somewhat conflicting agendas. An irresistibly catchy organ riff and Kate's delicate vocal dominates the first minute, until Prince's rush of sound enters and grabs centre stage with both hands, with the three-piece brass section and the Trio Bulgarka also on the cast list.

As Prince had not recorded the backing vocals Kate had wanted, they found another performer, closer to home—Lenny Henry. Though better known as a comedian, he had made several solo singles during the previous fifteen years and was therefore no stranger to the recording studio. She sent him a tape, he learnt his parts, and then she gave him some additional coaching—something she had obviously not managed with The Purple One. When he arrived at the studio, he told her the guitar sounded 'so much like Prince—was that what you were going for?' 'It sounds like Prince because it IS him,' was the reply. 'Do you wanna go in the booth?' He sang his heart out, scarcely able to believe that he was performing on a song with two of his heroes.[9] Del used some compression on his work afterwards to make it sound 'a little more throaty'.

An earlier demo version, about ninety seconds longer, appeared on the internet almost twenty years later.

12. 'You're the One' 5.53

The album's final and longest track, stretching to almost six minutes, is another ballad about the end of a relationship, yet another piece that seemed to be places Kate's music nearer mainstream pop and rock, closes the album. It is a song full of lament, of regret about what might have been. Soul-baring lines like 'I'm going to stay with my friend/Mmm, yes, he's very good-looking/The only trouble is, he's not you', suggest a saddened lover's self-pity. It reaches a dramatic climax with 'Just forget it, all right! Everything I have I bought with you/Everything I do we did together'.

Perhaps significantly, it is not Danny who contributes guitar alongside the rhythm section. Gary Brooker again adds some haunting Hammond organ and Kate plays Fender Rhodes, but this time it is Jeff Beck on guitar who joins a small but select roll call of musical heavyweights, while Trio Bulgarka again add backing vocals.

It might have been a mournful tune, but Kate still allows herself (and the listener) a gentle in-joke. About two minutes before the end, as it winds to a stately conclusion with Beck's guitar solo and Brooker's haunting Procol Harumesque organ, she slips in a line referencing the first verse of the latter group's classic 'A Whiter Shade of Pale'—'We tied ourselves in knots, doing cartwheels 'cross the floor'.

Aerial

UK: Released 7 November 2005, EMI, No. 3

US: Released 2005, Columbia, No. 48

Personnel: Kate Bush: vocals, keyboards (1–3, 5, 6, 8, 10, 13–16) piano (4, 7, 9, 12)

Dan McIntosh: electric and acoustic guitar (1, 2, 5, 6, 10, 12, 14–16)

Del Palmer: bass guitar (1, 5, 6, 14, 16)

Paddy Bush: backing vocals (1)

Steve Sanger: drums (1, 16)

Stuart Elliott: drums (2, 5, 12, 14)

Eberhard Weber: electric upright bass (2, 9)

Lol Creme: backing vocals (2, 15)

Eligio Quinteiro: renaissance guitar (3)

Richard Campbell, Susanna Pell: viol (3)

Bill Thorp: string arrangement (3)

Robin Jeffrey: renaissance percussion (3)

Chris Hall: accordion (5)

Michael Wood: male vocal (7)

Albert McIntosh (Bertie): 'The Sun' (8), 'The Painter' (10, 11, in 2018 reissue)

Peter Erskine: drums (9, 10, 15)

London Metropolitan Orchestra: strings (9, 11)

Michael Kamen: orchestral arranger and conductor

John Giblin: bass guitar (10, 12, 15)

Rolf Harris: 'The Painter' (10, 11), (not in 2018 reissue), didgeridoo (11)

Gary Brooker: backing vocals (12, 14), Hammond organ (14, 15)

Bosco D'Oliveira: percussion (15, 16)

Recorded at Abbey Road Studios, 1996–2004

Produced by Kate Bush

Although there was to be a twelve-year hiatus before the next release, Kate had spent part of this time writing and recording new material, as well as enjoying a well-earned sabbatical out of the public eye, largely so she could enjoy the benefits of a normal private family life with Dan and their son, Albert ('Bertie'). Preceded in October 2005 by the single 'King of the Mountain', entering a world in which physical singles were becoming increasingly supplemented if not supplanted by downloads, the eagerly-anticipated *Aerial* was released in the following month and entered the British album chart at No. 3. Like *The Red Shoes*, it did not feature a cover photograph of its creator, but instead one that was emblematic of the album's celebration of sky, sea, and birdsong. The image, looking at first glance like a rock formation or mountain range at sunset reflected on the sea, was later revealed to be a waveform of a blackbird song superimposed over a glowing photograph of sunset. The title, concealing several meanings, was chosen to suggest not only height and flight, but also antennae for sending and receiving—and maybe, it was hinted with tongue in-cheek (and indifferent spelling), the washing powder that Mrs Bartolozzi, the leading character in one particular track, might have used.

Once again, the musical content of the album was nothing if not eclectic. Musically it spanned elements of folk, classical, Renaissance, reggae, flamenco, and rock, with lyrics dwelling on such themes as her own family and domestic life, Elvis Presley, and mathematics. As with *Hounds of Love*, it was divided into two distinct halves, lasting thirty-eight minutes and forty-two minutes respectively. The first disc, *A Sea of Honey*, featured a set of seven unrelated songs including the single 'King of the Mountain'.

The second disc, *A Sky of Honey*, consisted of a single connected, conceptual piece of music tracing the arc of an entire day through nine interlinked pieces of music. On subsequent issues five years later, it became one continual track. In 2018, she reissued it as one of a series of her remastered albums on her label Fish People, and *A Sky of Honey* reverted to its original eight tracks. Also on this release, following his conviction for sexual offences four years earlier, Rolf Harris's spoken contributions to 'An Architect's Dream' and 'The Painter's Link' were removed and replaced by the voice of Albert 'Bertie' McIntosh.

In one of his final projects before he died in 2003, Michael Kamen arranged the string sections, performed by the London Metropolitan Orchestra.

When the record was completed, she invited Tony Wadsworth and Brian Munns from EMI to listen to it in its entirety. There was initially some discussion as to whether it should be released as a double album or two single ones a few months or even a year apart. She preferred the former idea, as it seemed fairer to her fans and better value to issue it as a double, and also as the music was completed she wanted to make it available all at the same time, regarding it as a unified piece of work physically and musically.

Tracks—Disc 1: *A Sea of Honey*

1. 'King of the Mountain' 4.53

Played for the first time in Britain on BBC Radio 2 on 21 September 2005, the only track released as a single (7-inch picture disc and CD only, with a drawing by Albert used as the artwork) entered and peaked in the UK singles chart at No. 4, Kate's first Top 5 hit for twenty years and her third-highest ever singles chart placing, and a high of No. 6 on the UK download chart. The only track on the album that sounded remotely like an obvious 45, even by Kate's decidedly uncommercial styles, it had been written and a demo recorded in 1996. A song about fame, isolation, and possible redemption, it was inspired by the theory that Elvis Presley, a reclusive modern-day Citizen Kane, could still be alive, watching the world from a mountain top and ready to rise again.

The song also has references to Citizen Kane, the fictitious newspaper magnate of the Orson Welles film reputedly based on William Randolph Hearst and others, to illustrate her thoughts on fame, wealth, and isolation. 'Why does a multi-millionaire fill up his home with priceless junk?' she asks in the first verse, and then a little later on with a hint of the Presley drawl, 'Elvis are you out there somewhere, looking like a happy man?' Was there an analogy between them and herself, she having been leading a relatively secluded existence enjoying her freedom away from the public eye for over a decade? That was for the listener to decide. She did, however, reveal in an interview not long after the record's release that she did not think human beings were 'really built to withstand that kind of fame'.

Musically, there is a hint of reggae in the rhythm, underpinned by bass guitar, although less obviously than 'Kite' on the first album, with a wash of almost ghostly synths as wind was heard in the background ('the wind is whistling in the house,' she intoned in one chorus). This continues for the first minute or so until the drums kick in, joined later by Del's guitar that starts as rhythm reggae before being unleashed into a scorching fury towards the end.

The drums were played by American jazz musician Peter Erskine and added to the previously recorded backing track. He chose to contribute a beat close to that of Weather Report's 'Nubian Sundance', a double tempo, free-syncopated, fairly aggressive style, and then added a Ringo Starr-style pattern as a counter point. When Del came to mix it, Peter said it sounded like Ron Tutt, who had been drummer with Elvis Presley's touring band. She looked at him with surprise, as she told him that was what the song was all about. Having not picked up on her lyrics because he was concentrating so intently on his playing, or her Elvis impersonation, he said he had no idea, but the tune had conveyed it subliminally to him.[1]

The B-side, recorded eleven years earlier, was her version of Marvin Gaye's 'Sexual Healing' (see p. 123).

2. 'p' 6.09

Talk about being top of the class at mathematics. Popular music never went more into the realms of *University Challenge* than track two, the tale of a 'sweet and gentle sensitive man with an obsessive nature and deep fascination for numbers, and a complete infatuation with the calculation of Pi', as the title is generally written. Some of the lyrics comprise rows of digits, as she sings the number to its 78th decimal place, then from its 101st to its 137th decimal place. At one time, a regular joke in music journalism was that the test of a good singer was 'so-and-so has such an amazing voice that he or she can even sing the telephone directory and make it sound good'. Here, Kate takes the analogy to new technological heights. She said she loved the challenge of singing numbers, as opposed to words, 'because numbers are so unemotional as a lyric to sing', and it was 'fascinating that there are people who actually spend their lives trying to formulate pi; so the idea of this number, that, in a way is possibly something that will go on to infinity'.[2]

Not long after the album's release, one fan claimed online that, much as he loved the track, her calculations were not completely accurate, and mused as to whether he could get her to re-record the figures correctly. Some people have frighteningly high IQs.

Musically, the song is underpinned throughout by Kate's keyboards, backed by the ever-reliable Stuart Elliott on drums and Eberhard Weber's bass, with Dan's acoustic rhythm guitar well in the background, and Lol Creme on backing vocals. Perhaps fortunately, Kate's vocal is relatively unobtrusive, and for the less mathematically-minded, it is quite possible to pass over the subject matter if required.

3. 'Bertie' 4.18

'Here comes the sunshine, here comes that son of mine', runs the opening line in a madrigal of unashamed maternal devotion. It was perhaps inevitable that, almost from her early days of stardom, Kate would be asked about her plans for having a family, and how would she combine having children and a career at the same time. She insisted that she could not imagine doing both at the same time. The birth of her son, Bertie, was the main reason she put her music on hold for a while. Such an important person would inevitably be celebrated in song on the next album that she made. Bertie, she said, was 'such a big part of her life … [and] a very big part of my work.' As he would not be young for very long, she wanted to make sure she did not miss out on his childhood and spent as much time with him as she humanly could: 'So the idea was that he would come first, and the record would come next, which is also one reason why it's taken a long time'. When she came to record the song she had written about him, she 'wanted to try and give it an arrangement that wasn't terribly obvious, so [she] went for the sort of early music'.[3]

Lest anybody found such a concept unduly mawkish, there were precedents for celebrating a young child on a comeback album. The most notable was John Lennon's 'Beautiful Boy (Darling Boy)', about his son, Sean, on *Double Fantasy*, issued in 1980 shortly before his untimely death.

The result is a Renaissance-style ode, performed with period instruments. Kate chose Susanna Pell and Richard Campbell, whom she had seen at a performance of St Matthew's Passion at Festival Hall, to play gamba, a renaissance period viol and distant cousin of the guitar, alongside classical guitarist Eligio Quinteira. She laid down a basic track the previous day with vocals and dulcimer. The other musicians then overdubbed their contributions, playing from notation that arranger Bill Dunne had provided. Eligio added his guitar overdub after they did the gamba track, reasonably close to chamber music, and Robin Jeffrey supplied percussion. Campbell recalled that Bertie himself even 'bounced into the studio at one stage while they were playing'.

4. 'Mrs Bartolozzi' 5.58

Another glimpse of life at home with the McIntoshes comes, more or less, in one of two songs featuring Kate just accompanying herself on piano. This tells of a lady who spends hours scrubbing her hall carpet and then cleaning the kitchen floor one wet day after her family had trodden mud all over the house, and then, one imagines, occupying much of her time doing the laundry. Mrs Bartolozzi was not Kate herself, she insisted—but she did spend a lot of her time washing, especially once she became a mother. She was pleased that so many people found it funny, as she thought it was 'one of the heaviest songs' she had ever written.

Clothes in themselves, she thought, were very interesting, being rather like people without the people in them, 'still having our scent, and pieces of us on them'. From that, it was only a step away to the idea of a woman in her house with her washing, the idea of these clothes tumbling around in the water, the water becoming the sea, and finally the sense of a journey, 'where you're sitting in front of this washing machine, and then almost as if in a daydream, you're suddenly standing in the sea'.[4] From the laundry to the sea is by any standards an imaginative connection. Even the clothes had a vaguely erotic connection: 'My blouse wrapping itself around your trousers'.

5. 'How to Be Invisible' 5.32

A moody, restrained instrumental backdrop of guitar, bass, and drums, punctuated with occasional notes on Chris Hall's accordion, accompanies Kate's ruminations on keeping out of the glare of publicity, and empowering oneself to become invisible. In the chorus, she considers everyday items that might be considered totally private—eye of braille, hem of anorak, stem of wallflower, and hair of doormat.

The title also gave itself to a book of Kate's lyrics, published in 2018.

6. 'Joanni' 4.56

Joanni is Joan of Arc, the fifteenth-century French heroine and saint put to death during the Hundred Years' War. The lyrics describe her on the battlefield, while the cannon are firing, the swords are clashing, the horses are charging and the bells are ringing. Musically, it is accompanied by a smooth wash of keyboards and Fairlight percussion, with some unobtrusive guitar and touches of sampled pan pipes-like sounds. Everything is very restrained, where one might have expected the subject matter—in which there is no narrative, and no reference to her capture or her fate beyond that—to call for something a little more dramatic.

7. 'A Coral Room' 6.12

Arguably the most moving six minutes on the entire album, this is a tribute to Kate's mother. There is no instrumentation here apart from her piano, which opens softly as she sings of dreaming about a city that becomes a scene of battle, with planes crashing down and pilots drowning. The scene then becomes a room, with only her mother and a little brown jug: 'It held her milk, and now it holds our memories'. This relates to recalling her mother singing a refrain from the old nineteenth-century American folk song, 'Little brown jug, don't I love thee'. Some likened the lyric to part of T. S. Eliot's *The Waste Land*, in which one of the characters was briefly taken back to her childhood, a carefree age soon to be banished by the onset of war. Kate confirmed that the song was about the passing of time, as she liked the idea of 'coming from this big expansive, outside world of sea and cities into, again, this very small space where it's talking about a memory of my mother and this little brown jug. I always remember hearing years ago this thing about a sort of Zen approach to life, where, you would hold something in your hand, knowing that, at some point, it would break, it would no longer be there.'[5]

The performance is completely solo, apart from a brief vocal interlude at the 'little brown jug' reference by Michael Wood.

Tracks—Disc 2: *A Sky of Honey* (Original Release and 2018 Remaster); *An Endless Sky of Honey* (2010 Release)

As on *Hounds of Love*, Kate followed a sequence of standalone songs with a full song cycle, *A Sky of Honey*. This time, in a suite of seven unashamedly romantic and interconnected songs, it takes the listener on a long day's journey into night, with the unfolding of a summer sky from dawn to dusk in music of pagan rapture, consisting of songs about acts of creation, natural or otherwise; about the wind, rain, sunlight, and sea; and on through to the next morning when birdsong is heard once more and the whole cycle begins all over again. Some parts just feature Kate alone at her piano, singing with restraint; on others, such as 'Sunset', she begins alone softly, then the tempo quickens and they become experiments in different genres, touching jazz, progressive rock, or flamenco. Significant parts of the soundtrack are provided by the song of wild birds, in her words, 'almost as if they're vocalising light', and adding that she loved the idea of it being a language humans did not understand. Each song refers to the sky and sunlight, with the sea also featuring as an important element. Reviewer Darren Waters likened the suite's rural feel to that of a poem by John Betjeman or A. E. Housman, and suggested that it was the kind of album Pink Floyd might have made if Kate had been their lead singer and lyricist in 1979.[6]

In the Before the Dawn concerts, she performed 'King of the Mountain' in an extended form, 'Joanni' and the Sky of Honey song cycle live for the first time.

8. 'Prelude' 1.26
An early morning awakening to a beautiful day of sunshine is heralded by a gentle wash of Fairlight, a dawn chorus of blackbirds and others, the soft 'whoo-whoo' of wood pigeons and a gentle wind in the trees give way to a gentle touch on the piano, with Bertie speaking. 'Mummy ... Daddy ... the day is full of birds ... sounds like they're saying words'.

9. 'Prologue' 5.42
The birdsong continues, although more in the background, as Kate sings with eagerness of a new summer day. She references George Meredith's *The Lark Ascending*, now better remembered after Ralph Vaughan Williams' musical setting, muses on the light in Italy, breaks into a few lines of Italian, and invites the listener to join her 'to find the song of the oil and brush'. Her piano is joined, sparingly, by Eberhard Weber's bass, Michael Kamen's orchestral arrangement, and a brief burst of Peter Erskine's drums towards the end—with a few seconds of birdsong after the final musical note.

10. 'An Architect's Dream' 4.50
The song is preceded by a pavement artist (Rolf Harris on the original, subsequently replaced by Bertie), thinking aloud about lightening and darkening the colours on his new landscape in progress. To a soft background of piano, Dan's guitar, John Giblin's bass, Peter Erskine's drums, and Kate's keyboards, she (or is it two lovers?) watches the painter at work while the light is changing. Then it starts to rain.

11. 'The Painter's Link' 1.35

To the pared-down sound of Michael Kamen's arrangement for strings, piano, and more birdsong follows a brief sequel. Rain is falling, the painter laments that his painting has fallen victim to the weather, and all his colours are running. But as Kate points out, there is a positive result: 'See what they've become—a beautiful sunset'.

12. 'Sunset' 5.58

What opens as another soft reflective piece—the sunset, as presaged by those running colours, 'could be honeycomb in a sea of honey'—as Kate sings with the piano, a hymn to the blackbirds that sing at dusk, picks up in tempo thanks to John Giblin's jazz-flavoured acoustic bass, and Stuart Elliott's drums, Latin American touches about halfway through, a visit to flamenco territory with Dan's guitar, and Gary Brooker returning on backing vocals before the end. The blackbird is granted the final note before it all segues into the next track.

13. 'Aerial Tal' 1.01

Can you imagine a chant in which Bertie—we assume it is her—duets with the blackbird, to a softly repeated rhythm on keyboard? A delightful way to spend sixty seconds.

14. 'Somewhere in Between' 5.00

Another shuffle with hints of a jazzy rhythm brings a subtle flavour to celebration of the ambiguous nature of dusk, as day turns into night—somewhere in between. The world, or rather its observers, now caught in a dream between sleeping and waking up; breathing out and breathing in; twilight is neither night nor morning. As well as Stuart Elliott's drums and Del's bass and Dan's guitar, Gary Brooker's Hammond organ joins in to shines once again as it approaches a final 'goodnight sun—goodnight mum'.

15. 'Nocturn' 8.34

Darkness has fallen, a midsummer night, with a New Age-style serenade to the approaching dawn. There are hints of two lovers driving into the moonlight under a star-studded 'diamond sky', perhaps in a dream, while their clothes lie on the beach and their footprints lead right up to the sea as they on the edge of the Atlantic. Meanwhile, against a sky of honey, the light is ever-changing, as they awake.

Joining Kate on keyboards are Dan on guitars, Peter Erskine on drums, John Giblin on bass, and Gary Brooker on Hammond organ again, with additional vocals from Lol Creme and percussion by Bosco D'Oliveira.

16. 'Aerial' 7.52

The song cycle returns to where it all began, at the start of a new summer's day, ending with an euphoric welcome to the next sunrise with the refrain 'I need to get up on the roof ... in the sun'. Kate joins the birds in their endless song (perhaps all that is missing is a cameo appearance from Bill Oddie), so a number with a pronounced beat. No, not quite disco, but you could be forgiven for allowing the thought to cross your mind. Then a little over two minutes in, the trilling of the birds is joined by almost uncontrollable laughter—say, it is all deliberate. She tried to think of anything in the language of *Homo sapiens* that was comparable to birdsong. The only thing that seemed to have any kind of natural connection was the way we laugh: '... there is something strangely connected in the shapes'. What could follow that? Two minutes in which Dan's almost frenzied rock guitar dominates a brisk percussive passage, until they fall silent—and only the birdsong remains, fading into the distance. As for the last twenty seconds of the track, to borrow a phrase—the rest is silence.

The band consists of Steve Sanger on drums, Del on bass, Dan on guitars, Kate on keyboards, and Bosco D'Oliveira on percussion.

11

Director's Cut

UK: Released 16 May 2011, Fish People, No. 2
US: Released 2011, Fish People, No. 186
Personnel: Kate Bush: vocals, keyboards, backing vocals, piano
           Paddy Bush: mandola, flute, whistle, backing vocals
           Steve Gadd: drums
           John Giblin, Eberhard Weber, Danny Thompson: bass guitar
           Danny McIntosh, Eric Clapton: guitar
           Gary Brooker: Hammond organ
           Albert McIntosh: programming, backing vocals
           Brendan Power: harmonica
           Ed Rowntree, Mica Paris, Jacob Thorn, Michael Wood, Jevan
           Johnson Booth: backing vocals
Recorded 2009–11
Produced by Kate Bush

Kate's follow-up to *Aerial*, and the first on her own record label, Fish People, consisted of songs that had originally appeared on *The Sensual World* and *The Red Shoes*. Three—'This Woman's Work', 'Rubberband Girl', and 'Moments of Pleasure'—were completely re-recorded, while the other eight were remixed and restructured while retaining most of the original instrumentation.

   As far as the other tracks were concerned, for some years she had planned to give songs on both albums a makeover, feeling they would benefit from minor changes at least. All lead vocals on the songs and some backing vocals were entirely re-recorded, with some of the songs transposed to a lower key to accommodate her altered range, and in every case making her sound a little more mature, lived-in, even dare one say it slightly more husky than before (compare the work of other male and female vocalists in their twenties and a few decades on—to give random examples, her hero Elton John, Bryan Ferry, Ray Dorset, or Bonnie Raitt). Apart from 'Rubberband Girl', these songs are longer than their originals—in some cases, by only a few seconds, sometimes a minute or more. The drum tracks were likewise re-recorded, featuring Steve Gadd. Also on the sessions were bassist Danny Thompson and backing vocalist Mica Paris.

Entering the chart at No. 2, it was available as a digital album, standard CD in a case-bound book, deluxe version (Collector's Edition), consisting of a box set including *Director's Cut*, *The Sensual World*, and *The Red Shoes* (remastered from digital to analogue), and two-disc vinyl. It was recorded using analogue equipment, as she had never liked the hard-edged sound of the digitally recorded *The Red Shoes*, and considered that both the new recordings of the songs from this album and the remastered *The Red Shoes* had a much warmer, fuller sound.

Tracks

1. 'Flower of the Mountain' 5.15

When Kate originally wrote 'The Sensual World', she had used some text from James Joyce's *Ulysses* and set it to a piece of music she had written, but was not granted permission to use it, much to her disappointment. While she still felt that the original words would have been better, in order to conform with copyright legislation, she had no choice but to rewrite it in her own lyrics. Some twenty years later, a second request to use Joyce's own work was granted, and she was free to record a new vocal using Molly Bloom's soliloquy. In the process, the song gained a new title, taken from the first verse of the song.

The new version is just over a minute longer, benefiting from the backing track being extended. On first listen, the new vocal sounds slightly detached from the instruments, although this may have been a deliberate effect to turn what had been a song into more of a half-spoken, half-sung soliloquy.

2. 'Song of Solomon' 4.45

A few seconds longer than the earlier version, while there is little difference in sound between the two, this has a warmer tone. As with the other tracks not re-recorded from scratch, the less crisp, more analogue tone is immediately evident and the instrumentation is slightly deeper in the mix, giving more prominence to Kate's vocal.

3. 'Lily' 4.05

As with the previous track, there is not much change from the original, apart from a warmer tone overall.

4. 'Deeper Understanding' 6.33

Kate's perceptive song on the relationship between a lonely person and a computer replacing human companionship now includes not only a newly-recorded main vocal, but also the voice of her son, Albert, on the chorus, playing the role of the computer program. In the process, it gains almost two minutes in length. An auto-tune effect was used on the chorus to represent the sound of the computer communicating, offering to 'bring you love and deeper understanding'. For the last two minutes, the laid-back shuffle of drums and bass, touches of harmonica and the computer that ultimately (and deliberately, one imagines) begins to malfunction until switching off of at the wall seems the only remedy take over until the fade. The effect might be akin to novelty but is effective nonetheless, although at the same time perhaps not something one would need to hear too often.

It was released as a digital download single on 5 April 2011, and reached No. 87 in the UK. Promotional CD singles were issued in different territories, including either the radio edit, album version, or both. Promotional DVDs also featured the video that she directed, starring Robbie Coltrane, Frances Barber, and Noel Fielding.

5. 'The Red Shoes' 4.58

Although the title track of the 1991 album was not re-recorded, the backing track was brought down to a lower pitch. While it retains its lively folksy flavour, there is a greater warmth and more power, and it feels a little looser, more spontaneous with the longer coda.

6. 'This Woman's Work' 6.30

The first of three songs re-recorded from scratch, and almost three minutes longer than the version on *The Sensual World,* this is for the most part a sparse number with just piano behind her vocals. The opening is reminiscent of soft notes twinkling from a music box bathed in echo, and for the last half of the number, her singing intrudes only very sparingly on a passage of luxurious velvet piano sounds, plus the ebb and flow of almost choral backing vocals, again from Albert McIntosh and Jacob Thorn—sometimes soft, sometimes more forceful—calling to mind the mood created by 10cc on 'I'm Not In Love'. Michael Kamen's orchestral arrangement is likewise delightfully unobtrusive while still lending the most subtle of colours to the palette. She admitted that this and 'Moments of Pleasure' felt like the most intimate tracks on the record, and the general consensus are that they are probably the best-liked.

7. 'Moments of Pleasure' 6.32

When Kate began work on a completely new recording of this most personal of songs, she admitted she did not know how it 'was going to come together', so she simply sat down and tried to play it again for the first time in about twenty years. She 'wanted to get a sense of the fact that it was more of a narrative now than the original version; getting rid of the chorus sections somehow made it more of a narrative than a straightforward song'.[1] In the process, she made it almost three minutes longer.

She often wrapped up the more personal elements of her songs behind literary references and character studies. For this one her almost conversational lyrics make the song come across like a more personal, intimate one-to-one with the listener, rather like thinking aloud. There are also slight alterations to the melody, she has dispensed with the strings, and the voices of the choir provide the only accompaniment to her voice and piano.

8. 'Never Be Mine' 5.05
On the original version, Kate's vocals began almost at once. This time round, the introduction lasts around thirty seconds before she starts to sing. Her voice is more relaxed, and the general production warmer, with the Trio Bulgarka less in evidence, not heard until near the end and even then further down in the mix than before.

9. 'Top of the City' 4.24
Despite the new lead vocal, a slight drop in pitch and a more analogue sound, this neither adds to nor subtracts significantly from the previous version.

10. 'And So Is Love' 4.21
Always an atmospheric, even sombre song, yet again the newer version only has minor differences, such as in the vocal phrasing towards the end, and with the line 'But now we see that life is sad' altered to 'But now we see that life is sweet'. Yet if anything it is slightly more chilling, with the backing vocals a little more buried in the mix, as are Eric Clapton's guitar lines.

11. 'Rubberband Girl' 4.37
If the original version startled some listeners with its good-time poppy vibe, the 2011 revisit would have amazed them even more. Kate and the group positively rock out here and had it not been for her singing, the first minute or so of rhythm guitar and Steve Gadd's drums would instantly have people reaching for comparisons with the Black Crowes or the Rolling Stones, either the groove of 'Street Fighting Man' or much of the material on the *Exile On Main Street* album (after all, the KT Bush Band were given to belting out 'Honky Tonk Women' in their pub rock days). Kate's unusually slurred vocal is hard to make out as she semi-does a Mick Jagger to Danny's Keith Richards-style rhythm guitar, not that it matters, and this time there are a few brief chord changes along the way. About three minutes in there is some extra flavour from the silvery keyboards, and rasping harmonica.

As with the 1993 model, it sounds like Kate is improvising to an extent in her vocal, as the musicians jam together until the final chord. It really does give the feeling that she and the other musicians have decided to let loose for once. On an artistic level, it may not be the record's crowning glory, but it is surely the most fun—possibly the most light-hearted track in her entire catalogue. Reviewer Helen Brown cited it as the 'best example on the record of Kate having stripped back the digital crunch of the production, giving the instrumentation more breathing space and creating a more intimate, organic feel', and suggesting that 'it [sounded] like it could have been recorded in the backroom of an Irish pub'.[2]

12

50 Words for Snow

UK: Released 21 November 2011, Fish People, No. 5
US: Released 2011, Fish People, No. 83
Personnel: Kate Bush: vocals (2–7), piano (1-3, 5, 7), backing vocals (1, 4),
           bass guitar (1), keyboards (4–6)
           Dan McIntosh: guitar (1, 3–6)
           Del Palmer: bass guitar (1), bells (4)
           Danny Thompson: double bass (3)
           John Giblin: bass guitar (4–6)
           Steve Gadd: drums (1–6)
           Albert McIntosh: featured vocal (1)
           Michael Wood and Stefan Roberts: featured vocal (2)
           Andy Fairweather Low: backing vocals (4)
           Elton John: featured vocal (5)
           Stephen Fry (as Prof. Joseph Yupik): featured vocal (6)
Recorded at Abbey Road Studios, 2010–11
Produced by Kate Bush

Nothing could convey the contrast more sharply between a glance at the front cover of this album and *Aerial*. The former with its glowing reds and golds instantly conveys an impression of summer sunshine, while its successor is one of softly-focused black, white, and grey, with two figures caressing and kissing each other for warmth against a background of ice in the depths of winter. 'It's not an album of pop songs,' she insisted, 'it's moving into a more grown-up world of music.'[1] Here are seven songs, all between six and fourteen minutes long, or rather pieces of sung and spoken word vocals and jazz-rock soundscapes (do not expect any conventional structures of verse-chorus-verse-chorus-bridge), 'set against a background of falling snow'. Two of them, at over ten minutes each, are the longest she ever committed to record. The title was inspired by her thoughts on the belief that the indigenous peoples of the northern circumpolar region have fifty words for snow.

For her it was a comparatively quick, easy record to complete, and very enjoyable to make as it was part of a continuing process. She recorded it very soon after completing *Director's Cut*, which had been a really intense record for them to make.

> When I finished it I went straight into making this so I was very much still in that focussed space; still in that kind of studio mentality. And also there was a sense of elation that suddenly I was working from scratch and writing songs from scratch and the freedom that comes with that.[2]

Each track is built around her subdued, often jazz-tinged piano and Steve Gadd's drumming, using both sung and spoken word vocals. The lengthy tracks are quite at odds with much of what she had done before, even further away from the mainstream, with sparingly used guitar supplementing a minimal rhythm section and electronics with the lightest touch. Pieces of music lasting seven minutes or more were allowed ample time to breathe and create an atmosphere, a soundscape, more free than ever before of conventional song structures, with not one but six additional vocalists—her son, two of her lifelong inspirations from the music world with successful careers reaching back to the late 1960s, a renowned actor, comedian, author, and broadcaster in one, and two choral singers. Some welcomed the deployment of different voices on the album, but not all. One reviewer called the duet with Elton John and the spoken word appearance from Stephen Fry the album's two 'duff notes', commenting that their voices were 'too meaty and familiar to be free to float in Bush's ethereal snow-globe world'.[3]

When it entered the UK album charts at No. 5, it gave her the distinction of being the first female recording artist to have an album of all new material in the Top 5 during each decade from the 1970s onwards.

Two stop-motion animation videos were released online to promote the album, one to accompany a section of 'Misty', the other for 'Wild Man'. A third followed a few weeks later, a black-and-white shadow puppet animation, 'Eider Falls at Lake Tahoe'.

As ever, the critical reception was universally favourable. Some reviewers commented how Kate had long been 'a prime inspiration for tech-savvy young auteurs [who had] pioneered the use of digital samplers in the 1980s and [was] still an avid aural manipulator', or on her extraordinary combination of jazz and classical minimalism, while others commented on 'the warm huskiness of her voice' in contrast to her albums of thirty years earlier, and compared it to similarly ground-breaking works by the likes of Joni Mitchell, Eno, and Scott Walker. Another, Alexis Petridis, commented that 'for all the subtle beauty of the orchestrations, there's an organic, live feel, the sense of musicians huddled together in a room, not something that's happened on a Bush album before'.[4]

Tracks

1. 'Snowflake' 9.52

The song telling of the birth of a snowflake and its journey from the clouds to the ground or into a human hand is sung over a soft, drifting ambient background of piano, Steve Gadd's sparing drums, Dan's occasional discreet guitar chords and Del's bass guitar, by Albert McIntosh, then just entering his teens, as an angelic choirboy. There are allegories to be found here. Some see it as the tale of a delicate snowflake embodying the hopes of a loud and busy universe about to be enveloped by snowfall and giving voice to the melting consciousness of the natural world itself. Others view it as a parable of mother and son, maybe human, or maybe Mother Earth and her creation; from the moment of birth the snowflake is engaged in a constant quest for his mother, while she sings softly to him: 'The world is so loud, keep falling, I'll find you'. At the same time, there is also a festive theme of nativity, in the line 'We're over a forest, it's midnight at Christmas'.

Kate particularly liked the idea of a snowflake, a fragile temporary creation, falling from the sky. Albert's high voice was likewise a fragile instrument that would not last for long before it dropped, and the meeting of both ideas struck her as a wonderful basis for a piece of music.

2. 'Lake Tahoe' 11.08

This eleven-minute epic was inspired by Kate's learning from a friend of the story relating to what is the largest alpine lake in the US. To this day, it is said, people occasionally see a woman who fell into the water during the Victorian era, then rises up and swiftly disappears once more. The freezing temperatures are credited with preserving her body. Kate is joined by choral singers Stefan Roberts and Michael Wood, fulfilling an idea she had long wanted to experiment with—using high male voices in contrast to her deeper tone. Together they sing of the ghost, appearing in a Victorian gown as she calls to her dog, Snowflake.

A 10-inch picture disc single was released for Record Store Day in 2012 in a limited edition of 2,000 copies, with 'Among Angels' on the B-side.

Kate wrote and directed a five-minute animated video, *Elder Falls at Lake Tahoe*, featuring shadow puppetry, to accompany the song.

3. 'Misty' 13.32

The album's longest track is a dark, surreal tale in which a young girl builds herself a snowman who comes to life. They spend a blissful night of passion together, ending inevitably with damp sheets as the ephemeral lover melts away. Kate admitted that it was partly about a sexual encounter, and that it was even 'a silly idea', but a tender one all the same. For much of the song, the only accompaniment is her piano, before Steve Gadd's drums, Danny Thompson's bass, and Dan's guitars help to heighten the dramatic atmosphere.

A short animated video, *Mistraldespair*, was released simultaneously with the album.

4. 'Wild Man' 7.17

The wild man is an elusive creature, otherwise known as the Kangchenjunga Demon, the Abominable Snowman, or the Yeti, whose cry can often be heard echoing around the mountainside. A group of people exploring the Himalayas find his footprints in the snow, and in order to protect him, they cover up the traces. He is urged to make himself scarce from his enemies: 'You were pulling up the rhododendrons, loping down the mountain … they will hunt you down, then they will kill you, run away, run away, run away'.

Guest vocals are supplied by Andy Fairweather Low, in the role of a Nepalese mountain-dweller. Kate had always been an admirer of his voice, from his early career as singer with Amen Corner, and when she wrote the song she decided he would fit perfectly. Dan's subtle guitar riff also supplies an atmospheric veneer to the sound.

Kate also had a message in that the song was also meant to be an empathetic view of a creature of great mystery. She felt strongly that 'mankind wants to grab hold of something [like the Yeti] and stick it in a cage or a box and make money out of it … I think we're very arrogant in our separation from the animal kingdom and generally as a species we are enormously arrogant and aggressive. Look at the way we treat the planet and animals.'[5]

A radio edit, lasting just over four minutes, was played on BBC Radio 2's Ken Bruce show on 10 October and a CD single, featuring both the radio edit and the album version, was released the next day. It spent one week in the British charts at No. 73. In 2015, a remixed version was included on *The Art of Peace: Songs for Tibet II* compilation album, also featuring tracks by Peter Gabriel, Sting, Howard Jones, Bob Geldof, and Elbow, celebrating the eightieth birthday of the Dalai Lama.

5. 'Snowed in at Wheeler Street' 8.05

One of Britain's most enduringly successful male vocalists at last gets the chance to add one of his most devoted protégées to the long list of partners with whom he has recorded duets, but this is as far away from the spirit of 'Don't Go Breaking My Heart' with Kiki Dee as one can imagine. Having long idolised Elton John's music, Kate wrote the song with him very much in mind, and was completely 'blown away by his performance on it'.

It is basically a time travel love song, in which a man and a woman regularly meet up at different times throughout the centuries. 'Excuse me, I'm sorry to bother you but don't I know you?' she asks at the start. 'There's just something about you, haven't we met before?' 'We've been in love forever,' he replies. They knew each other during the sack of Ancient Rome, when they got to the top of the hill and watched the city burning together, during the Second World War in 1942 when they found themselves on different sides, on 11 September 2001 in New York. They are clearly meant to be together, and have been in love for ever, but each time events conspire to pull them apart for a few more years, if not a few more centuries. At last they are reunited again, snowed in at Wheeler Street (maybe the one at Cambridge, maybe not—that is anyone's guess)—'just two old flames keeping the fire going, we look so good together'. 'Come with me, I'll find some rope and I'll tie us together,' she sings at one point. 'I've been waiting for you so long, I don't want to lose you again.'

A gentle keyboard pattern and rhythm section accompany both vocalists throughout, and only in the last two minutes or so, with the impassioned vocal trading of each, 'I don't want to lose you again', do the drums and cymbals build up to a climax.

6. '50 Words for Snow' 8.31

Many years earlier, Kate heard the theory that Inuits had fifty words for snow. She recognised it was a myth—but it made her think it was a great idea to have so many words for the same thing. The title track of the album therefore became a piece on which, against a shuffling rhythm section with a shuffling samba feel (think Rolling Stones again, think 'Sympathy for the Devil' but without the eerie 'hoo-hoo' chanting), with the rhythm section punctuated gently by guitar and keyboards, Professor Joseph Yupik (alias Stephen Fry) reads out fifty words, or rather terms, synonymous with the wintery down, while she keeps count and reminds him at intervals how many he still had to go.

'If you start actually thinking about snow in all of its forms you can imagine that there are an awful lot of words about it,' she thought. 'Just in our immediate language we have words like hail, slush, sleet, settling—so this was a way to try and take it into a more imaginative world.' Having decided on the basic idea for the song, she realised she needed 'someone who had an incredibly beautiful voice but also someone with a real sense of authority when he said things'. Her idea for the song, or rather narrative piece, 'was that the words would get progressively more silly really but even when they were silly there was this idea that they would have been important, to still carry weight.' She particularly wanted Stephen Fry to read them out and was delighted that he could do so: 'He just came into the studio and we just worked through the words. And he works very quickly because he's such an able performer'.[6]

Fry was astonished and flattered when his agent called him to ask whether he would like to record a track with Kate. With a laugh, he replied, 'there is only ever one possible answer, unless it's me singing. I said, "She does know I can't sing?"'[7]

Copyright restrictions do not permit the reproduction of song lyrics in print in their entirety without permission, so do not expect a complete list herewith. A small sample will have to suffice: drifting; twisting; whiteout; blackbird-braille; Wenceslasaire; eiderfalls; *phlegm-de-neige*; creaky-creaky; *crème-bouffant*; anechoic; blown-from-polar-fur; mistraldespair; and, finally, snow. Reviewer Will Hodgkinson was equivocal about the results, calling it 'an interesting idea, but it's more of a thespian's parlour game than a song'.[8]

7. 'Among Angels' 6.49

Kate performs the closing track with only her piano for accompaniment, a wistful love song with something of a Gershwinesque touch taken at such a leisurely pace that its two verses stretch out almost the entire length of the number—close on seven minutes. One reviewer suggested that her words read 'like the sweetest kind of suicide note'. A less downbeat interpretation might see or hear it more as a comforting homily from a friend in need, more on the lines of Carole King's 'You've Got a Friend', with its uplifting references to 'angels around you, they shimmer like mirrors in summer', and the reassurance in the final lines that 'There's someone who's loved you forever but you don't know it'.

The shortest track on the album, it was also the only one to be included in the setlist of the *Before the Dawn* concerts three years later.

The Other Sides

UK: Released 8 March 2019, Fish People, No. 18
Recorded 1975–2012
Produced by Andrew Powell, Jon Kelly, Kate Bush, George Martin, and
Michael Kamen

A compilation consisting largely of non-album A- and B-sides, this was initially
released on 16 and 30 November 2018 as part of the *Remastered* box set.
Available as two-CD or four-disc vinyl packages, they comprised her ten studio
albums plus four additional albums of remixes, B-sides, and rarities. These four
extra discs were subsequently issued separately as a standalone four-CD set.

Tracks—CD 1, 12-inch Mixes

'Running Up That Hill (A Deal With God)' (12" version) 5.49
'The Big Sky' (Meteorological Mix) 7.48
'Cloudbusting' (The Organon Mix) 6.36
'Hounds of Love' (Alternative Mix) 3.49
'Experiment IV' (Extended Mix) 4.50

Tracks—CD 2, The Other Side 1

'Walk Straight Down the Middle' 3.50
'You Want Alchemy' 4.21
'Be Kind to My Mistakes' 3.03
'Lyra' 3.19
'Under the Ivy' 2.10
'Experiment IV' (video version) 4.50

'Ne T'Enfuis Pas' (Kate Bush, Patrick Jeaneau, Vivienne Chandler) 2.34
'Un Baiser d'Enfant' 3.03
'Burning Bridge' 4.12
'Running Up That Hill (A Deal With God)' (2012 remix) 5.36

Tracks—CD 3, The Other Side 2

'Home for Christmas' 1.48
'One Last Look Around the House Before We Go' 1.04
'I'm Still Waiting' 4.28
'Warm and Soothing' 2.45
'Show a Little Devotion' 4.18
'Passing Through Air' 2.04
'Humming' 3.16
'Ran Tan Waltz' 2.47
'December Will Be Magic Again' 4.54
'Wuthering Heights' (New Vocal) 5.05

Tracks—CD 4, In Others' Words

'Rocket Man' (Elton John, Bernie Taupin) 5.02
'Sexual Healing' (Marvin Gaye, Odell Brown) 5.55
'Mná na hÉireann' (traditional) 2.58
'My Lagan Love' (traditional) 2.31
'The Man I Love' (George and Ira Gershwin) 3.19
'Brazil (Sam Lowry's First Dream)' (S.K. 'Bob' Russell, Ary Barroso) 2.15
'The Handsome Cabin Boy' (traditional) 3.15
'Lord of the Reedy River' (Donovan Leitch) 2.42
'Candle in the Wind' (Elton John, Bernie Taupin) 4.33

CD 2, The Other Side 1

'Walk Straight Down The Middle' 3.50

'You Want Alchemy' 4.21

This was written and recorded shortly after Kate completed *The Red Shoes* and *The Line, The Cross and the Curve*. It tells about walking in the hills one sunny afternoon, 'on a cloudbusting kind of day', and coming upon a beekeeper, a solitary man obsessed with his activity and tells her that his bees can change everything. 'You want alchemy, they turn the roses into gold, they turn the lilac into honey, they're making love for the peaches.' While her initial reaction is that he must be 'some kind of nut', she then begins to understand. One goes through life wondering if there are miracles, and then she comes face to face with one.

Musically it is a slow, dramatic number, with the Fairlight sampling strings and brass, dramatic gospelly backing vocals, and with quotations of Debussy's *Clair de lune* from *Suite bergamasque*. The song construction and her vocals owe a little something to Prince's 'Purple Rain'. It first appeared as an extra track on the European and Australian 'Eat the Music' CD singles in 1994.

'Be Kind to My Mistakes' 3.03

'Lyra' 3.19

Originally called 'Out of the Storm', this was written for the soundtrack of *The Golden Compass*, a 2007 fantasy adventure film based on *Northern Lights*, the first novel in Philip Pullman's trilogy *His Dark Materials*, and used over the closing credits. The introduction is based on that of a song that she originally wrote for the Walt Disney film *Dinosaur* in 2000 but was never used. Lyra Belacqua, the warlike figure of the title whose 'army stands behind her', is the heroine of the story.

A slow ambient song powered by the Fairlight with a mood similar to much of Enya's best-known work, it was recorded partly at Kate's home studio and partly at Abbey Road, featuring the Magdalen College Choir from Oxford University. Released in November 2007 as a download-only single from the soundtrack album, it reached No. 187 on the British chart. It was later nominated for the International Press Academy's Satellite Award for the best original song in a motion picture.

'Under the Ivy' 2.10

'Experiment IV' (video version) 4.50

'Ne T'Enfuis Pas' (Kate Bush, Patrick Jeaneau, Vivienne Chandler) 2.34

'Un Baiser d'Enfant' 3.03

'Burning Bridge' 4.12

'Running Up That Hill (A Deal With God)' (2012 remix) 5.36

CD 3, The Other Side 2

'Home for Christmas' 1.48

A short, sweet, and almost folksy song features only an acoustic guitar behind Kate's vocals, with the faint squeak of fingers moving up and down the strings on the fretboard to change chords adding a touch of intimacy. The only other instrument is a solo trumpet on the break.

It received its first airing in the BBC TV *The Comic Strip Presents* film *Wild Turkey*, shown on 24 December 1992. The following year, it was released as the B-side to 'Moments of Pleasure' in Britain and as B-side to 'Rubberband Girl' in America. She also released her own privately pressed 3-inch CD single in a Christmas card in December 1993.

'One Last Look Around the House Before We Go' 1.04

'I'm Still Waiting' 4.28

'Warm and Soothing' 2.45

'Show a Little Devotion' 4.18

This song deals with the common issue of one partner in a relationship asking 'what it is that you want'—by Kate's usual standards, an unusually straightforward theme. Prominent organ (suggesting a similarity to early Genesis) and electronic drums dominate the backing, with and a bass guitar well down in the mix. Recorded presumably during sessions for *The Red Shoes*, it had previously been a bonus track on the CD single of 'Moments of Pleasure' in Britain, and 'Rubberband Girl' in America.

'Passing Through Air' 2.04

'Humming' 3.16

The one song that made its first official appearance on record, and the oldest, caused no little excitement for the reason that it apparently paid tribute to one of the most influential of artists of all time, and whose death had cast a lasting shadow over the British music scene for months after it occurred. By this time, Kate was being a very selective interviewee, yet few people were in doubt as to the subject of this song that had probably been recorded as one of the historic 1975 demos but never travelled any further than as an eagerly sought-after bootleg until now. Also sometimes known as 'Maybe', it was apparently Kate's own homage to David Bowie, written after he announced the 'retirement' of his alter ego Ziggy Stardust at his Hammersmith Odeon concert on 3 July 1973, at which a fourteen-year-old Kate was in the audience.

Musically, it is a sprightly, country-tinged tune with the rhythm section supporting her on piano, and the guitar playing a riff rather like the piano figure that introduces Elton John's 'Tiny Dancer'. The opening line, 'You set the scene for any revolutionary who'll ferry me', is thought to be a cheeky reference to one of her other musical heroes, the singer who was at the time Bowie's main rival in the glam rock art pop stakes, Bryan Ferry. The subject of the lyrics is 'a rock singer too [who] may have many birds, and many songs for [his] morning', possibly a coded reference to his open first marriage to Angie.[1]

At any rate, it is a song of celebration, until the curtain falls with the closing line, 'But when you go there's nothing, there's nothing left'. Fans thought for a while that Bowie's announcement on stage that night was a genuine retirement, until it later became clear that it was nothing of the sort. Only after the momentous news of thirty-two years later did the world learn that there was 'nothing left'.

After his death, Kate was among those who paid tribute to the man who 'had everything [and] was intelligent, imaginative, brave, charismatic, cool, sexy and truly inspirational both visually and musically. He created such staggeringly brilliant work, yes, but so much of it and it was so good. There are great people who make great work but who else has left a mark like his? No one like him'.[2] While she had sometimes seemed only too ready to dismiss most of not all of her pre-1985 work, maybe her admiration for 'the Brixton boy' who had departed the stage for good persuaded her to sanction an official release for the song at last.

Fans had been given a tantalising audio glimpse long before. About fifty seconds of it were heard when Kate brought a rather lo-fi copy with her for an interview with Ed Stewart on Radio 1's *Personal Call*, in 1979. 'I was waiting for the flat note in the middle!' she laughed after it was faded out, but she did not add any further comments about the subject matter.

'Ran Tan Waltz' 2.47

'December Will Be Magic Again' 4.54

'Wuthering Heights' (New Vocal) 5.05

CD 4, In Others' Words

'Rocket Man' (Elton John, Bernie Taupin) 5.02

As Kate and Elton John had long been mutual admirers, it was hardly surprising— as well as a dream come true for her—that she should be asked to contribute to *Two Rooms*, an album by various artists covering his songs, among them The

Who, George Michael, Tina Turner, Eric Clapton, and The Beach Boys. Kate gave 'Rocket Man' a hint of a reggae beat, with uillean pipes. In an interview with Radio 1, she said that anybody who recorded cover versions had to try and make them really different from the original. The reggae treatment 'just seemed to happen … it just seemed to want to take off in the choruses'.[3]

The song was also noted as one of the last sessions, perhaps even the last, on which guitarist Alan Murphy ever played.

Released as a single, it reached No. 12 in the UK in December 1991. After Kate had performed it that month on Terry Wogan's TV show, the host sent her mother, Hannah, a 'get well soon' message on air, though sadly the latter died two months later. In 2007, a poll in the *Observer Music Monthly* voted it the best cover version of all time.

'Sexual Healing' (Marvin Gaye, Odell Brown) 5.55

Kate's version of the Marvin Gaye Top 10 hit from 1982 was initially recorded in 1994 for *A Place Among the Stones*, an album by Davy Spillane. He played uillean pipes on the recording, but the track was omitted as it was felt that it did not sit comfortably alongside the sound of the rest of the record. It was played at a 1994 Kate Bush fan club convention in London, but otherwise remained unheard until released as the B-side of her single 'King of the Mountain' in 2005. Pipes apart, Kate's own rendition follows and retains the seductive, laid-back mood of the original faithfully.

'Mná na hÉireann' (traditional) 2.58

In English, 'Women of Ireland', this started as a poem written by the Ulster poet Peadar Ó Doirnín in the eighteenth century, and was set to an air composed by Seán Ó Riada in the mid-twentieth. At the request of Donal Lunny, Kate recorded her version in 1995 for a compilation album *Common Ground: Voices of Modern Irish Music*, issued the following year.

Aware that she approached it at a slight disadvantage, not being an Irish speaker herself (even though half-Irish, saying with a smile that she was sure her mother gave her a helping hand), she listened to earlier recordings so she could be as faithful to the correct pronunciation as possible. At least one Irish reviewer was less than positive about her efforts, but others praised her for her passion and 'fiery interpretation'. Helping her out were Nollaig Ni Chathasaigh of the RTE National Symphony Orchestra on violin, and Laoise Kelly on Irish harp, and the Irish Studio Orchestra with strings arranged and conducted by Fiachra Trench

In performing the song, she joined a long and illustrious list of others, including Alan Stivell, Davy Graham, The Chieftains, Sarah Brightman, and Mike Oldfield, who had also recently recorded it themselves.

'My Lagan Love' (traditional) 2.31 – see p. xx – see p. xx

'The Man I Love' (George and Ira Gershwin) 3.19

Kate was one of several artists invited to sing material from the Great American Songbook for a tribute album of Gershwin songs, *The Glory of Gershwin*, celebrating the eightieth birthday of harmonica maestro Larry Adler in 1994. Others included Peter Gabriel, Sting, Chris de Burgh, Meat Loaf, Carly Simon, and Jon Bon Jovi with Richie Sambora, and the collection was produced at Abbey Road by George Martin. Kate gives a faithful rendition of the song to a tasteful easy listening jazz arrangement. Released as a single in July that year and credited jointly to Kate Bush and Larry Adler, it reached No. 27 in Britain.

'Brazil (Sam Lowry's First Dream)' (S. K. 'Bob' Russell, Ary Barroso) 2.15

The title song from a 1985 British-American dystopian sci-fi film directed by Terry Gilliam, this was originally recorded and produced by Michael Kamen, who scored the film, with Kate providing the vocals. This recording was not included in the actual film or the original soundtrack release, but subsequently appeared on reissues of the soundtrack. With its sumptuous string arrangement, it sounds like a number straight out of the golden age of Hollywood musical from the '30s or '40s.

'The Handsome Cabin Boy' (traditional) 3.15 – see p. xx

'Lord of the Reedy River' (Donovan Leitch) 2.42 – see p. xx

'Candle in the Wind' (Elton John, Bernie Taupin) 4.33

Originally the B-side of 'Rocket Man', Kate accompanied herself on another Elton John number just with keyboards and Fairlight, staying more closely to the original. An instrumental version was also featured on the CD version. First recorded by Elton on his album *Goodbye Yellow Brick Road* in 1973 and a No. 11 hit for him the following year (a live version reached No. 5 in 1988), it was his tribute to Marilyn Monroe, who had died in 1962. Taupin, who had written the lyrics, said the song was about the idea of fame or youth or somebody being cut short in the prime of their life. Was it not for the fact that Marilyn was specifically mentioned, it could have been about James Dean, Montgomery Clift, or Jim Morrison, as an epitaph about how the media idolises those who die young. In 1997, Elton gave the song a new lease of life, and in the process made what would be the best-selling single in British history by a mile, when it was re-recorded with altered lyrics as 'Candle in the Wind '97' in memory of Diana, Princess of Wales.

Endnotes

* Online sources; for full details and URL see Bibliography

All interviews are with Kate Bush unless stated otherwise

Introduction

1   Jovanovic, R., *Kate Bush* (Portrait, 2005), p. 56.
2   Napier-Bell, S., *Black Vinyl White Powder* (Ebury, 2002), p. 201.
3   Adams, T., 'Kate Bush: the return...' *The Observer*, 20 November 2011.
4   Radcliffe, M., Interview with Maddy Prior, BBC Radio 2, 24 July 2019.
5   Bruce, K., Interview, BBC Radio 2, 9 May 2011.
6   Reynolds, S., 'Kate Bush, the queen of art-pop ... ', *The Guardian*, 21 August 2014.
7   Power, E. and O'Connor, R., The 40 best song lyrics ...' *Independent*, 20 August 2019.
8   *The Kate Bush Story*, BBC TV documentary, 2014.

Chapter 1

1   Gill, A., 'Kate Bush - Return of the sensual woman'. *The Independent*, 22 April 2011.
2   Thomson, G., *Under The Ivy* (Omnibus, 2010), p. 90.
3   Sutcliffe, P., 'Labushka', *Sounds*, 30 August 1980.
4   Music Talk, 1978, quoted in Kate Bush Encyclopedia.
5   Jovanovic, R., *Kate Bush* (Portrait, 2005), p. 38.
6   'Kate Bush's first boyfriend reveals secret ...'. *Daily Mirror*, 24 September 2010.
7   Jovanovic, R., *op. cit.*, (Portrait, 2005), p. 51.
8   *Ibid.*, p. 63.
9   *Ibid.*, p. 62.
10 *Ibid.*, p. 64.
11 Doherty, H., 'The kick outside,' *Melody Maker*, 3 June 1978.
12 Thomson, G., *op. cit.*, p. 92.
13 Reynolds, S., 'Kate Bush, the queen of art-pop ...'. *The Guardian*, 21 August 2014.

14 *The Kate Bush Story*, BBC TV documentary, 2014.
15 Thorpe, V., 'Out on the wiley, windy moors...' *Observer*, 8 July 2018.
16 Aston, M., The essential Kate Bush in 10 records'. *Vinyl Factory*, 4 June 2015.
17 Sutcliffe, P., 'Labushka'. *Sounds*, 30 August 1980.

Chapter 2

1 Thomson, G., *Under The Ivy* (Omnibus, 2010), p. 115.
2 *Ibid.*, p. 117.
3 *Tracks*, November 1989.
4 *Lionheart* promo cassette, EMI Canada, 1978.
5 *Kate Bush Fan Club Newsletter*, Summer 1979.
6 *Ibid.*
7 *Lionheart* promo cassette, EMI Canada, 1978.
8 Doherty, H., 'Enigma Variations', *Melody Maker*, 11 November 1978.
9 Personal Call, BBC Radio 1, 2 August 1979.
10 *Ibid.*
11 *Kate Bush Fan Club Newsletter*, Summer 1979.

Chapter 3

1 *Kate Bush Fan Club Newsletter*, September 1980.
2 Peter Powell, interview, Radio 1, 11 October 1980.
3 Thomson, G., *Under The Ivy* (Omnibus, 2010), p. 165.
4 Needs, K., 'Fire in the bush', *Zigzag*, August 1980.
5 Thomson, G., *op. cit.,* p. 160.
6 Jewell, D., 'How to write songs and influence people,' *Sunday Times*, 5 October 1980.
7 Needs, K., *op. cit.*
8 Nicholls, M., 'Among the bushes,' *Record Mirror*, 12 July 1980.
9 Irwin, C., 'Paranoia and passion of the Kate inside,' *Melody Maker*, 10 October 1980.
10 Jewell, D., *op. cit.*
11 Needs, K., *op. cit.*
12 Irwin, C., *op. cit.*
13 Pearson, D., 'The me inside,' *Smash Hits*, May 1980.
14 Needs, K., *op. cit.*
15 *Ibid.*

Chapter 4

1 Thomson, G., *Under The Ivy* (Omnibus, 2010), p. 182.
2 Myatt, T., Interview, Kate Bush fan convention, November 1985.
3 Thomson, G., *op. cit.,* p. 189.
4 *Ibid.*, p.194-5.
5 Kate Bush Club Newsletter, October 1982.
6 J.J. Jackson, Interview, MTV, November 1985.
7 Thomson, G., *op. cit.,* p. 23.

8   Cloudbusting – Kate Bush in her own words.

9   Smith, R. 'Getting down under with Kate Bush.' 1982, journal unknown.

10 Cook, R., 'My music sophisticated?' *NME*, 16 October 1982.

11 J.J. Jackson, *op. cit.*

12 *Kate Bush Club Newsletter*, October 1982.

13 *Ibid.*

14 *Ibid.*

15 Simper, P., 'Dreamtime is over'. *Melody Maker*, 16 October 1982.

16 *Kate Bush Club Newsletter*, October 1982; Birch, I., 'What I did on my holidays.' *Smash Hits*, 23 July 1981.

17 *Kate Bush Fan Club newsletter*, October 1982.

18 Makowsky, J., 12 Essential Kate Bush songs, Popmatters, 17 September 2014.

19 Thomson, G., *op. cit.*, p. 191

Chapter 5

1   Sutherland, S., 'The Language of Love,' *Melody Maker*, 21 October 1989.

2   Lucas, J., Kate Bush: 10 of the best, *Guardian*, 27 August 2014.

3   Skinner, R., Radio 1 Classic Albums, interview, 26 January 1992.

4   *Guardian*, 23 November 2018.

5   *Kate Bush Club Newsletter*, October 1985.

6   *Ibid*; Myatt, T., interview, Kate Bush fan convention, November 1985.

7   Thomson, G., *Under The Ivy* (Omnibus, 2010), p. 214.

8   Skinner, R., *op. cit.*

9   *Ibid.*

10 *Ibid.*

11 Walters, B., *Hounds of Love*, review, *Pitchfork*, 12 June 2016.

12 Thomson, G., *op. cit.*, p. 217.

13 Skinner, R., *op. cit.*

14 *Ibid.*

15 *Ibid.*

16 *Ibid.*

17 *Ibid.*

Chapter 6

1   Thomson, G., *Under The Ivy* (Omnibus, 2010), p. 228.

2   *Ibid.*, p. 227.

Chapter 7

1   Scott, R., interview, Radio 1, 14 October 1989.

2   Brown, L., 'In the realm of the senses'. *NME*, 7 October 1989.

3   Horkins, T., 'What Katie did next.' *International Musician*, December 1989.

4   Brown, L., *op. cit.*

5   Scott, R., *op. cit.*

6   Horkins, T., *op. cit.*

7   *Ibid.*

8   Brown, L., *op. cit.,* Scott, R., *op. cit.*
9   Horkins, T., *op. cit.*
10 Scott, R., *op. cit.*
11 Dilberto, J, 'Kate Bush's Theater of the Senses'. *Musician*, February 1990.
12 Brown, L., *op. cit.*
13 Sutherland, S., 'The Language of Love'. *Melody Maker*, 21 October 1989.
14 Horkins, T., *op. cit.*
15 Brown, L., *op. cit.*
16 Horkins, T., *op. cit.*
17 Scott, R., *op. cit.*
18 Horkins, T., *op. cit.*
19 Brown, L., *op. cit.*

Chapter 8

1   Mellor, D., Interview with Ken Livingstone, LBC, 28 March 2014.

Chapter 9

1   *Mojo*, June 2011
2   Thomson, G., *Under the Ivy* (Omnibus, 2010), p. 254.
3   Jovanovic, R., *Kate Bush* (Portrait, 2005), p. 187.
4   Bruce, K, Interview, BBC Radio 2, 9 May 2011.
5   Jovanovic, R., *op. cit.*, p. 189.
6   Thomson, G., *op. cit.*, p. 252.
7   Jovanovic, R., *op. cit.*, p. 189.
8   *Ibid.*
9   Henry, L., 'Lenny Henry on Prince,' *Guardian*, 24 April 2016.

Chapter 10

1   Thomson, G., *Under The Ivy* (Omnibus, 2010), p. 294.
2   Bruce, K, Interview, BBC Radio 2, 31 October 2005.
3   *Ibid.*
4   *Ibid.*
5   Wilson, J., Interview, BBC Radio 4, 1 November 2005.
6   Waters, D., *Aerial*, review, BBC News online, 28 October 2005.

Chapter 11

1   Dombai, R., 'Kate Bush: The elusive art-rock originator...' Pitchfork, 16 May 2011.
2   Brown, H., *Director's Cut* review, *Daily Telegraph*, 13 May 2011.

Chapter 12

1 Pomfret, E., 'Clever pop?' *The Times*, 31 January 2012.
2 Doran, J., 'A demon in the drift ....' *The Quietus*, 21 March 2014.
3 Brown, H. *50 Words For Snow*, review, *Daily Telegraph*, 18 November 2011.
4 Petridis, A., *50 Words For Snow,* review, *Guardian*, 17 November 2011.
5 Doran, J., *op. cit.*
6 *Ibid.*
7 *The Kate Bush Story*, BBC TV documentary, 2014.
8 Hodgkinson, W., 'She's off to see the blizzard.' *The Times*, 18 November 2011.

Chapter 13

1 Pafford, S., 'Humming: Kate Bush's revolutionary song ...'. *Bowie News*, 1 December 2018.
2 *David Bowie, 'As remembered by...' Guardian, 17 January 2016.*
3 Walker, J., Interview, BBC Radio 1, 14 December 1991.

Bibliography

Books

Jovanovic, R., *Kate Bush: The Biography* (Portrait, 2005)
Juby, K., *Kate Bush: The Whole Story* (Sidgwick & Jackson, 1988)
Napier-Bell, S., *Black Vinyl White Powder* (Ebury, 2002)
Thomson, G., *Under the Ivy: The Life & Music of Kate Bush* (Omnibus, 2010, new ed. 2012)

Articles, Interviews, Reviews, and Documentaries

Adams, T., 'Kate Bush: the return of pop's most resonant voice.' *The Observer*, 20 November 2011
Birch, I., 'What I did on my holidays.' *Smash Hits*, 23 July 1981
Brown, H., *50 words for snow*, review, *Daily Telegraph*, 18 November 2011; *Director's Cut*, review, *Daily Telegraph*, 13 May 2011
Brown, L., 'In the realm of the senses.' *New Musical Express*, 7 October 1989
Bruce, K, Interviews, BBC Radio 2, 31 October 2005, 9 May 2011
Cook, R., 'My music sophisticated? I'd Rather You Said That Than Turdlike!' *New Musical Express*, 16 October 1982
Dilberto, J, 'Kate Bush's Theater of the Senses.' *Musician*, February 1990
Doherty, H., 'The kick outside.' *Melody Maker*, 3 June 1978; 'Enigma Variations.' *Melody Maker*, 11 November 1978
Doran, J., 'A demon in the drift: Kate Bush interviewed.' *The Quietus*, 21 March 2014
Doyle, T., 'I'm not some weirdo recluse.' *The Guardian*, 28 October 2005
Gill, A., 'Kate Bush - Return of the sensual woman.' *Independent*, 22 April 2011
Henry, L., 'Lenny Henry on Prince: "I almost passed out. This was my hero talking to me."' *Guardian*, 24 April 2016
Hodgkinson, W., 'She's off to see the blizzard.' *The Times*, 18 November 2011
Horkins, T., 'What Katie did next.' *International Musician*, December 1989
Irwin, C., 'Paranoia and passion of the Kate inside.' *Melody Maker*, 10 October 1980
Jackson, J. J., Interview, MTV, November 1985
Jewell, D., 'How to write songs and influence people.' *Sunday Times,* 5 October 1980

'Kate Bush's first boyfriend reveals secret of famous song.' *Daily Mirror*, 24 September 2010

'Love, trust and Hitler.' *Tracks*, November 1989

Lucas, J., 'Kate Bush: 10 of the best.' *Guardian*, 27 August 2014

Myatt, T., Interview, Kate Bush fan convention, November 1985

Needs, K., 'Fire in the bush.' *Zigzag*, August 1980

Nicholls, M., 'Among the bushes.' *Record Mirror*, 1980 [full date not known]

Pearson, D., 'The me inside.' *Smash Hits*, May 1980

Petridis, A., 'Kate Bush—every single ranked!' *Guardian*, 23 November 2018

Pomfret, E., 'Clever pop? It's a long story.' *The Times*, 31 January 2012

Powell, P. Interview, BBC Radio 1, 11 October 1980

Power, E. and O'Connor, R., 'The 40 best song lyrics, from Kendrick Lamar to Nirvana.' *Independent*, 20 August 2019

Radcliffe, M., Interview with Maddy Prior, BBC Radio 2, 24 July 2019

Reynolds, S., 'Kate Bush, the queen of art-pop who defied her critics.' *The Guardian*, 21 August 2014

Ross, G., 'Kate Bush playlist: The enduring 40-year fascination of this artist's work.' *Independent*, 30 July 2018

Scott, R., Interview, BBC Radio 1, 14 October 1989

Simper, P., 'Dreamtime is over.' *Melody Maker*, 16 October 1982

Skinner, R., Classic Albums, BBC Radio 1 interview, 26 January 1992

Smith, R. 'Getting down under with Kate Bush.' 1982, journal unknown

Stewart, E., Personal Call (Interview), BBC Radio 1, 2 August 1979

Sutcliffe, P., 'Labushka.' *Sounds*, 30 August 1980

Sutherland, S., 'The Language of Love.' *Melody Maker*, 21 October 1989

Thorpe, V., 'Out on the wiley, windy moors, Kate Bush sings new praises to Emily Brontë.' *Observer*, 8 July 2018

Walker, J., Interview, BBC Radio 1, 14 December 1991

Wilson, J., Interview, BBC Radio 4, 1 November 2005

Other Journals

Kate Bush Club/Fan Club Newsletters
Mojo
Record Collector
Uncut

Online and Miscellaneous Material (Accessed January–October 2019)

Aston, M., 'The essential Kate Bush in 10 records'. *Vinyl Factory*, 4 June 2015, thevinylfactory.com/features/the-essential-kate-bush-in-10-records/

Cloudbusting—Kate Bush in her own words, gaffa.org/cloud/music/there_goes_a_tennor.html

Dombai, R., 'The elusive art-rock originator on her time-travelling new LP, *Director's Cut*.' *Pitchfork*, 16 May 2011, pitchfork.com/features/interview/7968-kate-bush/

Hewitt, B., 'Moments of Pleasure: *The Red Shoes* By Kate Bush 25 Years On.' The Quietus, 15 October 2018, thequietus.com/articles/25478-the-red-shoes-kate-bush-anniversary-feature-review

Kate Bush Encyclopedia, www.katebushencyclopedia.com

Kate Bush Story, The, BBC TV documentary, 2014

Lionheart, promo cassette, EMI Canada, 1978

Makowsky, J., 12 Essential Kate Bush songs. *Popmatters*, 17 September 2014, www. popmatters.com/12-essential-kate-bush-songs-2495616334.html

Pafford, S., *Humming*: Kate Bush's revolutionary song about David Bowie is finally released. *Bowie News*, 1 December 2018, stevepafford.com/bushbowie/

Reaching Out, 1978 interview transcript, gaffa.org/reaching/im78_tki.html

Walters, B., *Hounds of Love,* review, *Pitchfork*, 12 June 2016, pitchfork.com/ reviews/albums/21964-hounds-of-love/

Waters, D., *Aerial*, review, BBC News online, 28 October 2005, news.bbc.co.uk/1/hi/ entertainment/music/4386346.stm

Websites

Allmusic: www.allmusic.com

Discogs: www.discogs.com

Official charts: www.officialcharts.com/

45cat: www.45cat.com